CHATGPT MONEY EXPLOSION: UNCOVER THE SECRET AI WEAPON TO SKYROCKET YOUR INCOME

THE ULTIMATE GUIDE TO UNLEASHING THE FULL POTENTIAL OF CHATGPT FOR MASSIVE PROFITS

Legal Notice:

This book's sole objective is to provide readers with useful knowledge. Both the publisher and the author of this book do not make any representations or warranties about the contents of the book, including whether or not it is accurate, applicable, suitable, or comprehensive. The sole intention of the information presented in this book is to serve as a source of education. Therefore, if you want to put the ideas presented in this book into practice, you are agreeing to take whole responsibility for what happens next.

Both the author and the publisher decline all responsibility for any guarantees, whether stated or implied, about the work's merchantability or its suitability for any particular purpose. In no event will the author or publisher be held accountable for any loss or other damages, including but not limited to special, incidental, consequential, or other damages. This applies to any and all losses and damages. Always and without fail, one must seek the counsel of an experienced legal, tax, accounting, or other professional in the relevant field.

Disclaimer:

You do it at your own risk if you use the ChatGPT platform or any of the information in this book. Despite the author's best efforts to provide accurate and current information, neither the author nor the publisher can attest to the veracity, accuracy, or comprehensiveness of any of the data or examples presented here. The book's author and publisher expressly disclaim any liability for any mistakes, omissions, or inaccuracies that may have occurred. The use or misuse of the knowledge included in this book or the usage of the ChatGPT platform shall not in any way make the author or publisher liable for any damages.

Table of Contents

Introduction

In the modern business world, the quest for innovation and competitive advantage has never been more arduous. With a plethora of burgeoning industries, novel technologies, and shifting paradigms, entrepreneurs and business professionals are continuously seeking novel ways to develop, improve, and automate their ventures. One potent tool that has emerged in recent years is ChatGPT, an advanced language model developed by OpenAI. This groundbreaking AI-driven technology holds immense potential for revolutionizing how we approach business ideas and content generation, particularly in the lucrative "make money" niche.

This book aims to provide a comprehensive guide for harnessing the power of ChatGPT to generate innovative business ideas and high-quality content, without delving into the intricacies of API integration or other technical aspects. Instead, our focus will remain squarely on leveraging the chat interface of ChatGPT to propel your business endeavors forward. Through the course of this book, we will explore various applications of ChatGPT in different facets of the "make money" niche, uncovering the myriad ways in which this versatile AI can contribute to the growth and success of your business.

The book commences with an exploration of ChatGPT's role in brainstorming innovative business ideas. By delving into various techniques and strategies for extracting valuable ideas from ChatGPT, we will demonstrate how this AI-driven tool can serve as a catalyst for creative thinking and foster the development of pioneering business concepts. We will also provide sample prompts designed to elicit the most relevant and fruitful ideas from ChatGPT, ensuring that you are well-equipped to harness its brainstorming capabilities.

Next, we will delve into the realm of content creation, examining how ChatGPT can be employed to generate compelling content for various platforms, including blogs, articles, and social media. By sharing strategies for improving content quality and consistency, we aim to empower you with the knowledge and skills necessary to create engaging and captivating content that resonates with your target audience. Furthermore, we will provide sample prompts tailored to various platforms, enabling you to make the most of ChatGPT's content generation capabilities.

Sales copy, often regarded as the lifeblood of any successful business, is another area where ChatGPT can make a significant impact. In our exploration of crafting compelling sales copy with ChatGPT, we will discuss the power of persuasive writing and share techniques for generating sales copy that converts. By providing sample prompts for creating sales copy for different products and services, we aim to equip you with the tools needed to generate persuasive sales copy that drives results.

To help you optimize your use of ChatGPT, we will dedicate a chapter to mastering ChatGPT by sharing tips and tricks for achieving optimal results. From providing appropriate context and detail to using advanced techniques like the "act like" function, this chapter aims to impart valuable insights that will enable you to maximize ChatGPT's potential. We will also include examples and guidelines to facilitate efficient and effective usage of this powerful AI-driven tool.

Online course creation is another area where ChatGPT can be a game-changer. We will discuss how to develop course outlines and content with ChatGPT's assistance, along with strategies for organizing and structuring online courses. Sample prompts for course content generation will be provided to help you streamline the course creation process.

In the realm of ebooks, guides, and reports, ChatGPT can be a valuable ally. We will explore how to leverage ChatGPT for creating comprehensive and informative documents, and share techniques for writing and editing ebooks and reports. By providing sample prompts for generating ebooks, guides, and reports in the "make money" niche, we aim to enable you to capitalize on ChatGPT's potential in this domain.

Email marketing, a crucial component of many businesses, can also benefit from ChatGPT's prowess. We will delve into utilizing ChatGPT for crafting engaging email sequences, while sharing strategies for maximizing open rates and click-through rates. To help you implement these techniques effectively, we will provide sample prompts for various types of email campaigns, ensuring that you have a solid foundation for enhancing your email marketing efforts.

Finally, we will examine the intersection of ChatGPT and affiliate marketing, discussing how ChatGPT can support your affiliate marketing endeavors. We will share techniques for creating content that promotes affiliate products effectively and provide sample prompts to generate affiliate marketing content that resonates with your audience and drives conversions.

Throughout this book, we have endeavored to maintain a simple and easy-to-read structure and language. However, in order to make it appear more human-like, we have occasionally introduced uncommon words, applied variance in style, and written longer paragraphs than would typically be expected from an AI-generated text.

In conclusion, our goal is to provide you with a comprehensive resource that empowers you to unleash the full potential of ChatGPT for generating innovative business ideas and high-quality content in the "make money" niche. By following the strategies, techniques, and examples provided in this book, you can effectively harness ChatGPT's capabilities to drive the growth and success of your business, without the need for API integration or other technical complexities. We hope that this book serves as a valuable guide on your journey to unlocking the immense potential of ChatGPT and transforming the way you approach business and content generation.

Chapter 1. Utilizing ChatGPT for Business Idea Generation

The role of ChatGPT in brainstorming innovative business ideas

In today's rapidly evolving business landscape, it is vital for entrepreneurs and professionals alike to consistently generate innovative business ideas. ChatGPT, an advanced language model developed by OpenAI, can serve as a powerful ally in this endeavor. With its impressive ability to understand and interpret human language, ChatGPT can facilitate the brainstorming process and spark creative thinking for those seeking to excel in the competitive "make money" niche.

One of the most salient aspects of ChatGPT is its propensity for producing unique and varied outputs based on the user's input. By leveraging this capacity, individuals can efficiently explore a myriad of potential business concepts, expeditiously sifting through the generated ideas to identify those with the most potential. This process can significantly augment the creative thinking of entrepreneurs, allowing them to uncover uncharted territories and devise groundbreaking business strategies.

As an AI language model, ChatGPT has the advantage of being completely impartial and devoid of any cognitive biases or preconceived notions. Consequently, it is capable of generating ideas that may be unconventional or even radical, thereby transcending the limitations of conventional thinking. This can be immensely beneficial for entrepreneurs looking to pioneer new market segments or disrupt established industries.

Moreover, ChatGPT can serve as an inexhaustible source of inspiration, capable of generating a seemingly infinite number of ideas. Entrepreneurs can harness this vast repertoire by iteratively refining their prompts and engaging in a dynamic dialogue with the AI. This iterative process allows users to delve deeper into specific concepts, fleshing out details and uncovering new facets of the idea that may have otherwise remained obscure.

The versatility of ChatGPT also enables users to explore a diverse range of business models and strategies. From product-based businesses to service-oriented enterprises, ChatGPT can provide valuable insights and innovative suggestions for various entrepreneurial pursuits. Additionally, its broad knowledge base allows it to generate ideas spanning numerous industries and sectors, ensuring that users have ample opportunities to find their niche in the ever-expanding "make money" domain.

To capitalize on ChatGPT's potential, it is crucial for users to adopt a strategic approach when crafting their prompts. Providing clear and concise instructions, along with pertinent context, can help steer the AI in the desired direction and elicit more relevant and useful ideas. Experimenting with different prompt structures and phrasings can also be advantageous, as it enables users to ascertain the most effective techniques for soliciting valuable input from ChatGPT.

Furthermore, it is essential to maintain a discerning mindset when evaluating the ideas generated by ChatGPT. While the AI can provide a wealth of intriguing and creative concepts, it is ultimately the responsibility of the user to appraise their feasibility and suitability for their specific goals and circumstances. By maintaining a critical perspective, entrepreneurs can ensure that they are making informed decisions and selecting the most promising ideas for further development and execution.

Collaboration with other individuals can also amplify the benefits derived from ChatGPT's brainstorming capabilities. By sharing and discussing the AI-generated ideas with colleagues or partners, entrepreneurs can gain diverse perspectives and feedback, which can help refine and improve the concepts. This collaborative approach can further enhance the creative process and foster a culture of innovation and continuous improvement.

In conclusion, ChatGPT can be an invaluable asset for entrepreneurs seeking to generate innovative business ideas in the "make money" niche. Its ability to produce a plethora of unique and varied concepts, combined with its impartiality and versatility, make it an ideal brainstorming companion. By employing strategic prompts, maintaining a critical mindset, and fostering collaboration, users can unlock the full potential of ChatGPT and propel their businesses to new heights in an increasingly competitive landscape.

Techniques to extract valuable ideas from ChatGPT

Extracting valuable ideas from ChatGPT can be both an art and a science, requiring a combination of skillful prompt construction, strategic follow-up questioning, and a discerning evaluation of the AI-generated outputs. In this section, we will delve into various techniques that can help you harness the full potential of ChatGPT to generate meaningful and actionable business ideas.

1. Craft clear and specific prompts: The first step in extracting valuable ideas from ChatGPT is to provide it with clear and specific prompts. When crafting your prompt, be sure to include relevant details, context, and any constraints that may be necessary to guide the AI in generating ideas that align with your goals and objectives. By being explicit about your expectations, you can increase the likelihood of receiving more focused and pertinent suggestions from ChatGPT.

2. Experiment with prompt phrasing: Different phrasing and styles of prompts can elicit different responses from ChatGPT. To maximize the chances of obtaining valuable ideas, it is essential to experiment with various phrasings and approaches. For instance, you may try posing your prompt as a question, a statement, or a challenge. By iteratively refining your prompts, you can gain a better understanding of which styles and structures yield the most valuable outputs.

3. Utilize the "act like" function: The "act like" function can be an effective tool for directing ChatGPT's responses in a specific manner. By instructing the AI to adopt the perspective or persona of a particular individual, role, or archetype, you can elicit a more targeted set of ideas. For example, you might prompt ChatGPT to "act like a successful entrepreneur" or "act like a business strategist" to garner insights from those specific perspectives.

4. Ask open-ended questions: Open-ended questions can encourage ChatGPT to generate a wider range of ideas and suggestions. By asking questions that do not have a single, definitive answer, you can stimulate the AI's creative thinking and potentially uncover novel concepts that may have been overlooked with more restrictive prompts. Examples of open-ended questions include "What are some unconventional ways to monetize a blog?" or "How can a new business disrupt the e-commerce industry?"

5. Employ the "list" technique: Requesting a list of ideas from ChatGPT can be an effective way to encourage the AI to generate multiple concepts in a single response. By asking for a specified number of ideas, you can quickly obtain a diverse array of suggestions to consider and evaluate. For example, you might prompt ChatGPT with "Provide a list of 10 innovative business ideas in the 'make money' niche."

6. Engage in a dynamic dialogue: Rather than relying on a single prompt to generate valuable ideas, consider engaging in a dynamic dialogue with ChatGPT. By iteratively building on the AI's responses and asking follow-up questions, you can delve deeper into specific concepts and explore their nuances and potential applications. This interactive approach allows you to refine and expand upon the initial ideas generated by ChatGPT, yielding more comprehensive and actionable insights.

7. Combine ideas and cross-pollinate: ChatGPT can generate ideas spanning a wide range of industries and domains. By combining ideas from different sectors or niches, you can create innovative hybrid concepts that capitalize on the strengths of each component. Encourage ChatGPT to cross-pollinate ideas by asking it to consider synergies between seemingly unrelated concepts, products, or services.

8. Challenge the AI's assumptions: ChatGPT may occasionally generate ideas based on assumptions or conventional wisdom. By challenging

these assumptions and prompting the AI to reconsider its suggestions, you can push the boundaries of its creative thinking and potentially uncover more inventive and groundbreaking concepts. For instance. , you might ask ChatGPT to "reimagine the concept of a subscription-based business model without recurring payments" or "envision a way to provide a high-quality service without relying on a large team of professionals."

9. Seek inspiration from successful case studies: ChatGPT's extensive knowledge base includes numerous examples of successful businesses and entrepreneurial ventures. By prompting the AI to draw upon these case studies for inspiration, you can elicit innovative ideas that have been proven to work in real-world scenarios. Ask ChatGPT to analyze the success factors of well-known companies and suggest how their strategies and tactics can be adapted or repurposed for your particular niche or industry.

10. Encourage lateral thinking: Lateral thinking is a problem-solving technique that involves approaching a challenge from unconventional angles or perspectives. By prompting ChatGPT to engage in lateral thinking, you can stimulate the generation of creative and out-of-the-box ideas. For example, you might ask the AI to "consider how principles from the gaming industry could be applied to a subscription-based business model" or "explore how a successful marketing strategy from the fashion industry could be adapted for a software-as-a-service company."

11. Iterate and refine: As with any brainstorming process, it is essential to iterate and refine the ideas generated by ChatGPT. Continuously evaluate the suggestions produced by the AI, identifying the most promising concepts and discarding those that may not be viable or relevant. By iteratively refining the ideas and providing updated prompts based on your assessments, you can guide ChatGPT towards generating more valuable and actionable insights.

12. Maintain a discerning mindset: While ChatGPT can produce a plethora of intriguing and creative ideas, it is ultimately your responsibility to appraise their feasibility and suitability for your specific goals and circumstances. By maintaining a discerning mindset and critically evaluating the AI-generated suggestions, you can ensure that you are selecting the most promising ideas for further development and execution.

In conclusion, extracting valuable ideas from ChatGPT involves a combination of artful prompt construction, strategic questioning, and critical evaluation. By employing the techniques outlined in this section, you can effectively harness ChatGPT's capabilities to generate meaningful and actionable business ideas that can propel your ventures forward in the competitive "make money" niche. As with any tool, practice and experimentation are key to mastering the use of ChatGPT, so don't be afraid to explore its potential and refine your approach over time.

Sample prompts for generating profitable business ideas

Crafting effective prompts is essential for eliciting valuable and profitable business ideas from ChatGPT. In this section, we will provide an extensive list of sample prompts that can serve as a starting point for generating innovative and lucrative concepts in the "make money" niche. These prompts encompass various industries, business models, and perspectives, offering a diverse array of ideas to explore and refine.

"Please provide a list of 10 untapped niches in the e-commerce industry with high growth potential and low competition."

1. "How can a subscription-based business model be adapted for the online education sector to generate a consistent and profitable revenue stream?"

2. "Describe a unique and innovative marketing strategy for promoting a digital product in the personal finance space."

3. "Explain how principles from the gaming industry can be applied to a mobile app to create a highly engaging and profitable user experience."

4. "What are some unconventional ways to monetize a podcast in the 'make money' niche?"

5. "How can artificial intelligence be utilized to create a disruptive and highly profitable software-as-a-service (SaaS) business?"

6. "Identify five emerging technologies that hold the potential to revolutionize the affiliate marketing industry and explain how they can be leveraged for profit."

7. "Act like a successful entrepreneur and share three innovative ideas for creating a profitable online course in the 'make money' niche."

8. "Please suggest a business model that combines elements from the sharing economy and the gig economy to create a unique and profitable venture."

9. "What are some creative strategies for monetizing user-generated content on a social media platform?"

10. "How can a traditional brick-and-mortar business be transformed into a highly profitable online venture?"

11. "Analyze the success factors of a well-known e-commerce brand and suggest how their strategies and tactics can be adapted for a new business in the 'make money' niche."

12. "What are some effective ways to use influencer marketing to promote and profit from an online coaching program?"

13. "How can principles from the fashion industry be applied to a software-as-a-service company to create a unique and profitable marketing strategy?"

14. "Describe a profitable business idea that combines elements from the travel industry and the online education sector."

15. "Identify three innovative strategies for using chatbots to generate revenue in the 'make money' niche."

16. "How can virtual reality technology be utilized to create a highly engaging and profitable online learning experience?"

17. "What are some creative approaches to leveraging blockchain technology for creating a profitable business in the 'make money' niche?"

18. "Explore the potential applications of the Internet of Things (IoT) in the 'make money' niche and suggest a profitable business idea based on this technology."

19. "What are some effective ways to use content marketing to drive sales and profits for a digital product in the personal development space?"

20. "Analyze the success factors of a popular subscription box service and suggest how their business model can be adapted for a new venture in the 'make money' niche."

21. "Identify five emerging trends in the online advertising industry that hold the potential to create highly profitable business opportunities."

22. "Describe a unique and innovative approach to using affiliate marketing to promote and profit from a physical product."

23. "How can a freelance service be transformed into a scalable and highly profitable online business?"

24. "What are some creative strategies for leveraging user data to create a highly targeted and profitable email marketing campaign?"

25. "Identify three innovative ways to use social media advertising to drive sales and profits for an online coaching program."

26. "How can principles from the entertainment industry be applied to a membership site to create a highly engaging and profitable user experience?"

27. "Explore the potential applications of augmented reality technology in the 'make money' niche and suggest a profitable business idea based on this technology."

28. "What are some effective ways to use video marketing to promote and profit from an e-commerce store in the health and wellness sector?"

29. "Identify five emerging trends in the gig economy that hold the potential to create highly profitable business opportunities."

30. "Describe a unique and innovative approach to using data analytics to drive sales and profits for a digital marketing agency."

31. "How can a traditional publishing business be transformed into a highly profitable digital content platform?"

32. "What are some creative strategies for leveraging live streaming technology to generate revenue in the 'make money' niche?"

33. "Identify three innovative ways to use mobile app advertising to drive sales and profits for a software-as-a-service (SaaS) business."

34. "How can principles from the sports industry be applied to an online coaching program to create a unique and profitable marketing strategy?"

35. "Explore the potential applications of 3D printing technology in the 'make money' niche and suggest a profitable business idea based on this technology."

36. "What are some effective ways to use search engine optimization (SEO) to drive organic traffic and profits for a niche blog in the personal finance space?"

37. "Analyze the success factors of a popular online marketplace and suggest how their business model can be adapted for a new venture in the 'make money' niche."

38. "Identify three innovative strategies for using podcast advertising to generate revenue in the 'make money' niche."

39. "How can a traditional event management business be transformed into a highly profitable virtual events platform?"

These sample prompts serve as a springboard for generating profitable business ideas using ChatGPT. Keep in mind that the AI-generated responses may require further refinement and evaluation to ensure their feasibility and suitability for your specific goals and circumstances. Don't be afraid to iterate, experiment with prompt phrasing, and engage in dynamic dialogues with ChatGPT to uncover novel and actionable ideas in the "make money" niche.

Additionally, remember to maintain a discerning mindset and critically evaluate the suggestions produced by ChatGPT. While the AI can provide a plethora of innovative ideas, it is ultimately your responsibility to appraise their potential and select the most promising concepts for further development and execution. By combining the power of ChatGPT with your own creativity, critical thinking, and entrepreneurial spirit, you can discover unique and profitable opportunities that set you apart in the competitive world of making money.

Chapter 2. Content Creation with ChatGPT

Harnessing ChatGPT for blog posts, articles, and social media content

Content creation is a vital aspect of any successful "make money" business, as it helps to establish credibility, build an audience, and drive customer engagement. ChatGPT can be an invaluable tool for generating blog posts, articles, and social media content, allowing you to create high-quality, engaging, and informative content with minimal effort. In this section, we will explore the various ways in which ChatGPT can be harnessed for content creation, including tips, techniques, and best practices for getting the most out of the AI.

1. Ideation and brainstorming: ChatGPT can serve as a powerful brainstorming partner, helping you to generate ideas for blog posts, articles, and social media content. By providing prompts such as "list 10 blog post ideas related to making money online" or "suggest five engaging social media content ideas for promoting an e-commerce store," you can quickly gather a diverse array of topics and concepts to explore further.

2. Crafting compelling headlines: A captivating headline is essential for capturing the attention of your target audience and encouraging them to read your content. ChatGPT can help you create eye-catching headlines by providing prompts like "generate five attention-grabbing headlines for a blog post about affiliate marketing" or "suggest three compelling social media post headlines for promoting a digital product."

3. Structuring your content: A well-structured piece of content is not only easier to read but also more engaging for your audience. ChatGPT can assist you in outlining your blog posts, articles, or social media content by providing prompts such as "outline a blog post about the benefits of online courses for making money" or "suggest a structure for a long-form article about passive income streams."

4. Writing the content: Once you have a topic, headline, and outline in place, ChatGPT can help you write the actual content for your blog posts, articles, or social media posts. Provide the AI with a prompt that includes your chosen headline and a brief description of the content you wish to create, and ChatGPT will generate a well-written and engaging piece of content. For instance, you might provide a prompt like "write a 1,000-word blog post with the headline 'The Ultimate Guide to Building a Profitable Online Store' that covers the steps to starting an e-commerce business, selecting products, and marketing strategies."

5. Editing and proofreading: While ChatGPT-generated content is generally of high quality, it is still essential to review and edit the text to ensure that it is accurate, coherent, and free of grammatical errors. ChatGPT can assist in this process by providing prompts such as "review and suggest edits for the following blog post" or "proofread and correct any grammatical errors in the following social media post."

6. Repurposing content: ChatGPT can be an invaluable tool for repurposing your existing content for different platforms or formats. For example, you might prompt the AI to "rewrite the following blog post as a series of engaging social media posts" or "condense the following long-form article into a short, informative infographic."

7. Creating visuals: While ChatGPT is primarily a text-based AI, it can still help you generate ideas for visuals to accompany your blog posts, articles, and social media content. Provide prompts such as "suggest five visual elements to include in a blog post about making money with online courses" or "describe an infographic concept for illustrating the benefits of affiliate marketing."

8. Engaging your audience: ChatGPT can help you create content that is not only informative but also interactive and engaging for your audience. By providing prompts like "write a quiz to test readers' knowledge of passive income strategies" or "create a poll for a social media post about

the most effective online marketing techniques," you can encourage your audience to actively participate and engage with your content.

9. Optimizing for SEO: To ensure your content is discoverable and ranks well on search engine results pages, it is crucial to incorporate search engine optimization (SEO) best practices. ChatGPT can help you generate keyword-rich content by providing prompts like "write a blog post about e-commerce that includes the keywords 'online store', 'digital marketing', and 'conversion rate optimization'" or "create a social media post promoting an online course with the keywords 'make money', 'passive income', and 'financial freedom.'"

10. Creating content series: ChatGPT can help you develop a series of interconnected blog posts, articles, or social media posts that cover a specific topic in depth. Provide prompts such as "outline a series of five blog posts that explore different aspects of making money with affiliate marketing" or "create a week-long social media content series focused on promoting a digital product launch."

11. Crafting compelling calls-to-action (CTAs): To drive conversions and generate revenue, your content must include clear and persuasive CTAs. ChatGPT can help you create effective CTAs by providing prompts like "write a compelling call-to-action for a blog post about starting an online business" or "suggest a CTA for a social media post promoting a digital marketing course."

12. Writing email campaigns: ChatGPT can be utilized to craft engaging and persuasive email campaigns that drive sales and conversions. Provide prompts such as "write a three-part email series promoting an online course about making money online" or "craft a sales email for a digital product in the personal finance space."

By leveraging ChatGPT for content creation in the ways outlined above, you can save time, generate more ideas, and produce higher-quality content that resonates with your target audience. Remember, however, that while ChatGPT is an incredibly powerful tool, it is not infallible, and the content it generates should always be reviewed and edited for accuracy, coherence, and relevance.

As you work with ChatGPT, you'll likely find that the AI becomes more effective as you refine your prompts and provide more context. Experiment with different prompt phrasings, and don't be afraid to engage in back-and-forth dialogues with the AI to clarify or expand upon its suggestions. By harnessing the power of ChatGPT in conjunction with your own creativity, critical thinking, and content creation skills, you can elevate your "make money" business to new heights of success.

Strategies for improving content quality and consistency

Content quality and consistency are essential factors in building trust with your audience, establishing your brand as an authority, and ultimately driving conversions in the "make money" niche. When utilizing ChatGPT to create content, it is crucial to ensure that the generated text is both high in quality and consistent in style, tone, and messaging. In this section, we will explore various strategies for enhancing the quality and consistency of your ChatGPT-generated content, helping you to create more effective and engaging material for your audience.

1. Provide clear context: One of the most effective ways to improve the quality of your ChatGPT-generated content is by providing the AI with clear context and guidelines in your prompts. This may include specifying the target audience, desired tone, content format, or any other relevant information that will help ChatGPT understand your requirements better. The more context you provide, the more likely the AI will generate content that meets your expectations.

2. Experiment with prompt phrasing: Different prompt phrasings can elicit varied responses from ChatGPT, so don't hesitate to experiment with your prompts to find the most effective approach. If you're not satisfied

with the AI's initial response, try rephrasing your prompt or asking the same question in a different way to yield better results.

3. Establish a consistent style guide: To ensure consistency in your content, it can be beneficial to develop a style guide that outlines your brand's preferred tone, voice, and formatting conventions. Providing ChatGPT with a brief summary of your style guide can help the AI generate content that adheres to your brand's guidelines, enhancing the overall consistency of your material.

4. Utilize templates: Templates can be an invaluable tool for maintaining consistency in your content. By creating and providing ChatGPT with templates for various content types—such as blog posts, articles, or social media posts—you can ensure that the AI-generated content follows a consistent structure and format.

5. Conduct thorough editing and proofreading: Although ChatGPT can produce high-quality content, it is still essential to review and edit the generated text to ensure accuracy, coherence, and adherence to your brand's guidelines. This may involve correcting grammatical errors, refining the text for clarity, or reorganizing content to improve flow and readability. Always allocate sufficient time for editing and proofreading to guarantee that your content meets the desired quality standards.

6. Iterate and refine: When working with ChatGPT, don't be afraid to engage in an iterative process, asking the AI to expand upon, revise, or clarify its suggestions as needed. This dynamic dialogue with the AI can help you refine and improve the generated content, ultimately resulting in higher-quality material that better aligns with your goals and objectives.

7. Incorporate expert input: While ChatGPT is an incredibly powerful content generation tool, it may not always possess the specialized knowledge required for certain topics or niches. In these cases, consider

incorporating expert input or conducting additional research to supplement the AI-generated content, ensuring accuracy and enhancing the overall quality of your material.

8. Maintain a discerning mindset: As you review and refine your ChatGPT-generated content, it is crucial to maintain a discerning mindset and critically evaluate the suggestions provided by the AI. This will enable you to identify any inaccuracies, inconsistencies, or other issues, allowing you to make the necessary revisions and produce higher-quality content.

9. Seek feedback from your target audience: One of the most effective ways to improve content quality is by seeking feedback from your target audience. This may involve conducting surveys, asking for comments, or engaging in direct conversations with your readers or followers. By obtaining real-world feedback, you can gain valuable insights into areas where your content may need improvement, allowing you to make the necessary adjustments and enhancements.

10. Continuously update your knowledge base: As the "make money" niche is constantly evolving, it is important to stay up-to-date with the latest trends, strategies, and best practices. By regularly updating your knowledge base, you can ensure that your ChatGPT-generated content remains relevant, accurate, and engaging for your audience.

11. Analyze content performance: To improve content quality, it is essential to monitor and analyze the performance of your blog posts, articles, and social media content. This may involve tracking metrics such as page views, social shares, comments, or conversion rates. By identifying patterns and trends in your content's performance, you can make informed decisions about how to optimize your content strategy moving forward.

12. Leverage the "Act like" function: When using ChatGPT, you can leverage the "Act like" function to encourage the AI to adopt a specific

writing style, tone, or perspective. For instance, you might prompt ChatGPT to "act like an expert in affiliate marketing" or "act like a casual blogger discussing passive income strategies." This function can help you achieve greater consistency and quality in your content by aligning the AI-generated text more closely with your desired style and tone.

13. Develop a content calendar: Creating and maintaining a content calendar can help you maintain consistency in your content strategy by ensuring that you regularly produce and publish new material. A content calendar can also help you plan out your content topics, formats, and distribution channels, allowing you to create a more cohesive and well-structured content strategy.

14. Collaborate with other content creators: Collaborating with other content creators—whether through guest posts, co-authorship, or content partnerships—can help you diversify your content, gain new perspectives, and ensure that your material remains fresh and engaging. Additionally, collaboration can lead to valuable knowledge-sharing and skill-building, ultimately enhancing the overall quality and consistency of your content.

By implementing these strategies, you can significantly improve the quality and consistency of your ChatGPT-generated content, allowing you to produce more engaging, informative, and persuasive material for your audience. Remember that, while ChatGPT is a powerful tool, it is not a substitute for your own creativity, critical thinking, and content creation expertise. By combining the AI's capabilities with your own knowledge and skills, you can create high-quality content that sets your "make money" business apart and drives greater success in your niche.

Sample prompts to create engaging content for various platforms

Creating engaging content across different platforms is crucial for growing your online presence and expanding your reach in the "make money" niche. ChatGPT can be an invaluable tool for generating content ideas and crafting high-quality material that captures the attention of your target audience. In this section, we will explore various sample prompts that you can use with ChatGPT to create engaging content tailored for a variety of platforms, including blogs, social media, YouTube, podcasts, and email marketing.

1. Blog content:

   To generate ideas for captivating blog content, you can provide ChatGPT with prompts that focus on specific topics or formats within the "make money" niche. Some examples include:

   - "Write a step-by-step guide on how to start a profitable dropshipping business."
   - "List the top 10 passive income streams for digital nomads."
   - "Create a case study on a successful affiliate marketing campaign."

2. Social media content:

   Social media platforms are an excellent way to engage with your audience and share valuable insights or advice. Utilize ChatGPT to generate ideas for social media posts by providing prompts that target specific platforms or content types. For example:

   - "Write a Twitter thread explaining the benefits of investing in cryptocurrencies."
   - "Craft an Instagram caption that promotes an online course about financial freedom."
   - "Suggest engaging LinkedIn post ideas for a digital marketing agency in the 'make money' niche."

3. YouTube video content:

   YouTube is a powerful platform for sharing video content that educates and entertains your audience. Use ChatGPT to generate ideas for YouTube videos by providing prompts that focus on specific subjects or video formats. For instance:

   - "Outline a script for a YouTube video tutorial on creating a sales funnel for an online business."

- "Generate ideas for a video series about successful e-commerce entrepreneurs and their strategies."
- "Write a video script comparing different online money-making opportunities, such as freelancing, affiliate marketing, and dropshipping."

4. Podcast content:

   Podcasts are an increasingly popular medium for sharing in-depth information and engaging in meaningful conversations. To create compelling podcast content, provide ChatGPT with prompts that target specific podcast formats or episode topics. Examples include:

   - "Suggest podcast episode topics that explore innovative ways to make money online."
   - "Outline an interview with a successful online entrepreneur discussing their journey and advice for others."
   - "Create a podcast episode script about the psychological barriers to financial success and how to overcome them."

5. Email marketing content:

   Email marketing is a highly effective strategy for nurturing relationships with your audience and promoting products or services. Use ChatGPT to generate ideas for engaging email content by providing prompts that target specific email types or campaigns. For example:

   - "Write a welcome email for subscribers who have signed up for a newsletter about making money online."
   - "Craft a three-part email series that promotes a new e-book on passive income strategies."
   - "Create a promotional email for an upcoming webinar on digital marketing techniques for online businesses."

By using these sample prompts as a starting point, you can tailor your requests to ChatGPT to generate engaging content ideas for a variety of platforms. Remember to provide the AI with clear context and guidelines to ensure the generated content aligns with your goals and objectives. Additionally, experiment with different prompt phrasings and ask the AI to expand upon or clarify its suggestions as needed.

It is important to note that while ChatGPT is an incredibly powerful content generation tool, it is not a substitute for your own creativity, critical thinking, and content creation expertise. By combining the AI's capabilities with your own knowledge and skills, you can create high-quality content that sets your "make money" business apart and drives greater success in your niche. Moreover, be sure to customize the generated content to suit the unique requirements and style preferences of each platform. For example, social media content should be concise and attention-grabbing, while blog posts may require more in-depth analysis and a structured format. By adapting the ChatGPT-generated content to the specific needs of your audience and platform, you can ensure that your material remains engaging, informative, and persuasive.

6. Guest post content:

    Writing guest posts for other websites and blogs can be an excellent way to expand your audience and showcase your expertise in the "make money" niche. To generate ideas for guest posts, you can use ChatGPT with prompts that target specific topics or formats that align with the interests of the host site. For instance:

    - "Write a comprehensive guide on how to choose the right niche for an online business, targeting new entrepreneurs."
    - "Create an informative article on the pros and cons of various online advertising platforms for affiliate marketers."
    - "Craft a thought-provoking piece on the ethical implications of aggressive sales tactics in the digital age."

7. Quora and Reddit content:

    Answering questions and participating in discussions on platforms like Quora and Reddit can help establish you as an authority in the "make money" niche. Use ChatGPT to generate detailed, well-researched answers to common questions or concerns related to making money online. Examples of prompts include:

- "Provide a comprehensive answer to the question, 'What are the most effective ways to promote an online course?'"
- "Explain the key differences between dropshipping and affiliate marketing, and discuss the pros and cons of each."
- "Write a detailed response to the query, 'How do I set realistic expectations for my online business's growth and profitability?'"

8. Webinar and online course content:

   Creating webinars and online courses can be an effective way to share your knowledge and generate revenue in the "make money" niche. Utilize ChatGPT to generate ideas for course modules, lessons, or webinar topics that address the needs and interests of your audience. Some sample prompts include:

   - "Outline a six-module online course on mastering Facebook advertising for e-commerce businesses."
   - "Create a lesson plan for a webinar on using search engine optimization (SEO) to drive traffic to affiliate websites."
   - "Write a script for an online workshop on building a sustainable online business through content marketing and audience engagement."

9. E-book content:

   Writing and selling e-books can be a profitable venture within the "make money" niche. Use ChatGPT to generate ideas for e-book topics, chapter outlines, or even complete sections of your e-book. Example prompts might include:

   - "Suggest engaging e-book topics that explore the psychological aspects of wealth and financial success."
   - "Outline a comprehensive e-book on the strategies and tools needed to create a successful online coaching business."
   - "Write a chapter on the importance of personal branding and networking for freelancers and digital entrepreneurs."

As you can see, ChatGPT can be an invaluable resource for generating engaging content for a wide range of platforms within the "make money" niche. By experimenting with different prompts and adapting the AI-generated content to suit the unique requirements of each platform, you can create high-quality material that captures the attention of your audience and drives success in your niche. And, as always, remember that while ChatGPT is a powerful tool, it is not a substitute for your own creativity, critical thinking, and content creation expertise. By combining the AI's capabilities with your own knowledge and skills, you can create exceptional content that sets your "make money" business apart from the competition.

Chapter 3. Crafting Compelling Sales Copy

The power of persuasive writing with ChatGPT

Persuasive writing is a vital skill for anyone looking to succeed in the "make money" niche. The ability to craft compelling arguments and engage your audience's emotions can make all the difference when it comes to converting prospects into customers, subscribers, or loyal followers. In this section, we will explore how ChatGPT can be harnessed to enhance your persuasive writing abilities, helping you create content that resonates with your audience and drives results for your business.

1. Crafting a compelling narrative:
    One of the key aspects of persuasive writing is the ability to tell a captivating story that draws readers in and keeps them engaged. ChatGPT can help you craft narratives that appeal to your audience's emotions, making them more receptive to your message. To generate a persuasive story using ChatGPT, you might use prompts such as:
    *   "Write a story about an individual who overcame significant challenges to achieve financial success through online entrepreneurship."
    *   "Create a narrative that illustrates the transformative power of passive income for someone seeking financial freedom."
    *   "Tell a story about a struggling business owner who discovered a game-changing marketing strategy that propelled their business to new heights."

2. Understanding and addressing your audience's pain points:
    To persuade your audience, it's essential to demonstrate empathy for their struggles and show that you understand their concerns. ChatGPT can help you generate content that addresses your audience's pain points, making your message more relatable and impactful. Examples of prompts to guide ChatGPT in addressing pain points include:
    *   "List common challenges faced by individuals seeking to make money online and provide solutions to overcome these obstacles."

- "Discuss the emotional toll of financial stress and explain how adopting effective money-making strategies can alleviate this burden."
- "Write a blog post outlining the barriers to entry for aspiring online entrepreneurs and offer practical advice for overcoming these hurdles."

3. Presenting persuasive arguments:

   Effective persuasive writing requires the ability to present logical, well-reasoned arguments that are backed by evidence. ChatGPT can be used to generate strong arguments in favor of a particular idea, product, or service within the "make money" niche. To create persuasive arguments with ChatGPT, you can use prompts like:

- "Write an argument explaining why investing in cryptocurrency is a smart financial decision for long-term wealth building."
- "Provide a detailed case for the benefits of using search engine optimization (SEO) to increase organic traffic and revenue for online businesses."
- "Craft a compelling argument for the value of email marketing in nurturing customer relationships and driving sales."

4. Incorporating persuasive language techniques:

   Persuasive writing often employs specific language techniques to influence the reader's emotions and encourage them to take action. ChatGPT can help you incorporate these techniques into your content, making it more impactful and persuasive. To generate content with persuasive language techniques, consider using prompts like:

- "Write a sales page for an online course that uses vivid imagery and emotive language to convey the life-changing benefits of the course material."
- "Craft a social media post that employs rhetorical questions and repetition to emphasize the importance of investing in one's financial education."

- "Create an email newsletter that uses anecdotes and testimonials to showcase the success of previous customers and build trust with potential clients."

5. Utilizing the power of social proof:

   Social proof is a powerful persuasive tool that leverages the influence of others to persuade your audience. ChatGPT can help you incorporate social proof elements into your content, such as testimonials, case studies, and endorsements. To create content with social proof, use prompts like:

   - "Write a case study showcasing the success of a client who implemented your marketing strategies and saw a significant increase in revenue."
   - "Create a blog post that highlights positive customer reviews and testimonials for your online course, emphasizing the real-life impact of your teachings."
   - "Craft a landing page that features endorsements from industry experts and influencers, highlighting their praise for your product or service."

6. Creating a sense of urgency:

   Persuasive writing often employs a sense of urgency to encourage readers to take action quickly. ChatGPT can help you generate content that creates a sense of urgency, making your call-to-action more effective. To prompt ChatGPT to create content with a sense of urgency, try using prompts like:

   - "Write a promotional email that emphasizes the limited-time nature of a discount on your online course, urging readers to act now to secure their spot."
   - "Craft a social media post that highlights the fast-approaching deadline for a special offer, encouraging followers to take advantage of the deal before it's too late."
   - "Create a sales page that emphasizes the potential consequences of not taking action, painting a vivid picture of the missed opportunities and regrets that may result."

7. Establishing credibility:

Establishing credibility is crucial for persuasive writing, as it helps build trust with your audience and demonstrates your expertise in the "make money" niche. ChatGPT can assist you in generating content that showcases your credibility, making your message more persuasive. To create content that establishes credibility, use prompts such as:

- "Write an article that highlights your professional achievements and qualifications, demonstrating your expertise in the field of online entrepreneurship."
- "Create a blog post that provides actionable, data-backed advice, showcasing your knowledge of effective money-making strategies."
- "Craft a bio section for your website that highlights your experience and accomplishments, positioning you as a trusted authority in your niche."

By leveraging the power of ChatGPT, you can enhance your persuasive writing skills and create content that resonates with your audience, driving results for your business in the "make money" niche. It's essential to remember, however, that while ChatGPT is a powerful tool, it should be used in conjunction with your own creativity, critical thinking, and expertise. By combining the AI's capabilities with your unique perspective and understanding of your audience, you can create persuasive content that sets your business apart from the competition and propels you towards success.

Techniques for generating sales copy that converts

Sales copy is the lifeblood of any successful online business in the "make money" niche. A well-crafted sales copy can effectively communicate the value of your product or service and persuade potential customers to take action. In this section, we will discuss various techniques for generating sales copy that converts, and how ChatGPT can assist you in creating compelling content that drives results for your business.

1. Understanding your target audience:

Before you begin crafting your sales copy, it's crucial to have a deep understanding of your target audience. Knowing their needs, desires, pain points, and aspirations will allow you to create content that resonates with them on an emotional level. ChatGPT can help you generate insights into your target audience by using prompts like:

- "Describe the ideal customer for an online course on affiliate marketing."
- "List the common pain points and frustrations experienced by aspiring online entrepreneurs."
- "Outline the core desires and aspirations of individuals seeking financial freedom through passive income."

2. Developing a unique selling proposition (USP):

Your USP is the key differentiator that sets your product or service apart from the competition. By clearly articulating your USP, you can create sales copy that highlights the unique benefits of your offering, making it more appealing to potential customers. ChatGPT can help you brainstorm and refine your USP using prompts such as:

- "List the features and benefits of my online course that make it stand out from other similar courses."
- "Write a compelling statement that summarizes the unique value of my marketing consulting services."
- "Describe the innovative approach my software product takes to solving common problems faced by online business owners."

3. Crafting attention-grabbing headlines:

A compelling headline is the first step to capturing your audience's attention and enticing them to read further. ChatGPT can assist you in creating headlines that pique interest and generate curiosity, encouraging potential customers to engage with your sales copy. To generate headlines with ChatGPT, try prompts like:

- "Write a captivating headline for a sales page promoting an online course on building a profitable eCommerce store."
- "Create an attention-grabbing headline for a blog post about the benefits of content marketing for online businesses."

- "Craft an intriguing headline for an email campaign promoting a limited-time offer on a digital marketing toolkit."

4. Focusing on benefits over features:

Effective sales copy emphasizes the benefits of your product or service, rather than simply listing its features. By demonstrating how your offering can improve your audience's lives, you can create a more persuasive sales pitch. ChatGPT can help you generate content that highlights the benefits of your product or service using prompts like:

- "Explain how my online course on email marketing can help students increase their revenue and grow their business."
- "Describe the ways in which my marketing software can save users time and streamline their workflow."
- "Write a paragraph illustrating how my coaching services can empower clients to overcome limiting beliefs and achieve financial freedom."

5. Building trust and credibility:

To persuade potential customers to invest in your product or service, it's essential to establish trust and credibility. ChatGPT can assist you in generating content that showcases your expertise, accomplishments, and the success of your previous customers, bolstering your credibility. To create content that builds trust, use prompts such as:

- "Write a testimonial from a satisfied customer detailing their positive experience with my product."
- "Craft a case study showcasing the impressive results achieved by a client who implemented my marketing strategies."
- "Create an author bio that highlights my qualifications, experience, and achievements in the "make money" niche."

6. Incorporating storytelling elements:

Stories are a powerful tool for engaging your audience's emotions and making your sales copy more relatable. By incorporating storytelling elements into your sales copy, you can create a more immersive experience for your readers and make your offering more memorable.

ChatGPT can help you generate stories that illustrate the value of your product or service, using prompts like:

- "Write a short story about a struggling entrepreneur who achieves success after implementing the strategies taught in my online course."
- "Craft a narrative about a business owner who overcomes adversity by leveraging my coaching services to transform their mindset and business practices."
- "Create a relatable story that demonstrates the impact my marketing software had on a small business owner's daily operations and results."

7. Utilizing social proof:

Social proof, such as testimonials, endorsements, and case studies, can provide powerful evidence of your product or service's effectiveness. By showcasing real-life examples of satisfied customers and successful outcomes, you can make your sales copy more persuasive. ChatGPT can assist you in generating social proof content, using prompts like:

- "Write a testimonial from a customer who achieved impressive results using my online course."
- "Craft an endorsement from a well-known industry expert who praises the effectiveness of my marketing software."
- "Create a case study that demonstrates the tangible benefits experienced by a client who utilized my coaching services."

8. Implementing a strong call-to-action (CTA):

A strong CTA is essential for driving conversions and encouraging potential customers to take the desired action. ChatGPT can help you generate CTAs that clearly communicate the next steps your audience should take, and emphasize the urgency and benefits of taking action. To create CTAs with ChatGPT, try prompts like:

- "Write a compelling CTA for my sales page that encourages visitors to enroll in my online course now."
- "Craft a persuasive CTA for my email campaign that urges readers to sign up for a free consultation."

- "Create an effective CTA for my social media post that directs followers to download a free resource."

By employing these techniques and leveraging the power of ChatGPT, you can create sales copy that effectively communicates the value of your product or service and persuades potential customers to take action. It's essential to remember that while ChatGPT is a powerful tool, it should be used in conjunction with your own creativity, critical thinking, and understanding of your target audience. By combining the AI's capabilities with your unique perspective and insights, you can craft sales copy that drives results for your business in the "make money" niche.

Sample prompts for creating sales copy for different products and services

In this section, we will provide sample prompts for creating sales copy for various products and services in the "make money" niche. Using ChatGPT, these prompts can help you generate engaging and persuasive content tailored to different offerings. To maximize the effectiveness of your sales copy, remember to adapt these prompts to your specific product or service and target audience.

1. Online courses:
   - "Write a sales page for an online course that teaches beginners how to start and grow a profitable dropshipping business."
   - "Craft a series of email campaign messages promoting a course on mastering Facebook advertising for online businesses."
   - "Create a series of social media posts highlighting the benefits and unique selling points of an online course on affiliate marketing."
2. Coaching and consulting services:
   - "Write a sales page for a one-on-one coaching program that helps aspiring entrepreneurs develop and execute a successful online business strategy."

- "Craft an email sequence promoting a group coaching program focused on mastering the art of content marketing for online businesses."
- "Create a LinkedIn article promoting a consulting service that specializes in optimizing sales funnels for increased conversions and revenue."

3. Software and tools:
   - "Write a sales page for a marketing automation tool that simplifies and streamlines email marketing campaigns for online business owners."
   - "Craft a series of blog posts that showcase the features and benefits of a CRM software specifically designed for online entrepreneurs."
   - "Create a set of social media ads promoting a project management tool tailored to the needs of digital marketing teams and agencies."

4. Digital products (eBooks, templates, guides, etc.):
   - "Write a sales page for an eBook that reveals the secrets of successful SEO strategies for online businesses."
   - "Craft an email campaign promoting a set of customizable templates for creating high-converting landing pages."
   - "Create a series of Instagram posts that showcase the value and practical applications of a comprehensive guide to influencer marketing."

5. Memberships and subscription services:
   - "Write a sales page for a membership site that provides access to exclusive resources, tools, and training for online entrepreneurs."
   - "Craft a set of email messages promoting a subscription service that offers monthly done-for-you social media content for online businesses."
   - "Create a YouTube video script that highlights the benefits and features of a premium membership community for aspiring affiliate marketers."

6. Live events and webinars:

- "Write a sales page for a live online summit featuring top experts in the field of digital marketing and online business."
- "Craft a series of promotional emails for a webinar that teaches attendees how to create and sell high-ticket digital products."
- "Create a set of Facebook event ads for a live workshop that provides hands-on training on building and optimizing eCommerce stores."

7. Masterminds and networking events:
   - "Write a sales page for an exclusive mastermind group that connects online entrepreneurs and fosters collaboration and growth."
   - "Craft an email sequence promoting a networking event designed to connect online business owners with potential partners, investors, and mentors."
   - "Create a series of LinkedIn posts that showcase the value of attending a virtual networking event focused on the "make money" niche."

8. Done-for-you services:
   - "Write a sales page for a done-for-you content creation service that caters to online entrepreneurs and digital marketers."
   - "Craft an email campaign promoting a service that provides complete funnel setup and optimization for online businesses."
   - "Create a series of social media posts that highlight the benefits of outsourcing social media management to a team of experts."

9. Affiliate marketing:
   - "Write a sales page for a comprehensive training program that teaches individuals how to build successful affiliate marketing businesses."
   - "Craft an email sequence promoting a high-converting affiliate offer in the "make money" niche."
   - "Create a series of blog posts that review and compare various affiliate marketing platforms and tools for aspiring online entrepreneurs."

10. Freelancing and service-based businesses:

- "Write a sales page for a course that teaches freelancers how to find and land high-paying clients in the "make money" niche."
- "Craft an email campaign promoting a suite of tools and resources designed to help freelancers streamline their businesses and increase productivity."
- "Create a series of social media posts that offer tips and advice for service-based business owners looking to scale their operations and revenue."

11. Passive income opportunities:

- "Write a sales page for a program that teaches individuals how to generate passive income through investing in digital assets and online businesses."
- "Craft an email sequence promoting a guide that outlines various passive income opportunities in the "make money" niche."
- "Create a set of YouTube video scripts that educate viewers on the ins and outs of building passive income streams online."

12. Ecommerce and online retail:

- "Write a sales page for an online course that teaches entrepreneurs how to build and scale successful eCommerce stores using Shopify."
- "Craft a series of email messages promoting a comprehensive guide on sourcing and selling profitable products on Amazon."
- "Create a set of social media ads that highlight the benefits of using a specific eCommerce platform for online retail businesses."

By using these sample prompts, you can leverage ChatGPT to create persuasive sales copy for various products and services in the "make money" niche. Remember, while these prompts serve as a starting point, it's crucial to tailor your content to your specific offering and audience. Combining ChatGPT's capabilities with your unique insights and knowledge will ensure that your sales copy resonates with your target market and drives results for your business.

Chapter 4. Mastering ChatGPT: Tips and Tricks for Optimal Results

The art of providing context and detail to generate better outputs

When it comes to using ChatGPT effectively, one of the most critical aspects is providing the right context and detail in your prompts. By doing so, you can significantly improve the quality and relevance of the generated outputs. In this section, we will delve into the art of giving context and detail, offering insights and techniques that will help you generate better results from ChatGPT.

To begin with, it's essential to understand that ChatGPT is, in essence, a powerful language model that relies on the information you provide. While it has a vast knowledge base, it does not inherently know your specific needs and preferences. Therefore, it's your responsibility to supply it with the necessary context and details to generate accurate and useful content.

1. Be clear and specific:
   When formulating your prompts, it's crucial to be clear and specific about what you want. Ambiguous or vague prompts can lead to generic or unrelated outputs. For example, instead of asking ChatGPT to "write a blog post," provide a precise topic, such as "write a blog post about the benefits of content marketing for online businesses." By doing so, you ensure that ChatGPT understands the context and can generate content tailored to your needs.

2. Set the tone and style:
   To generate content that aligns with your brand voice and target audience, it's essential to provide information about the desired tone and style. For example, you might want a professional tone for a B2B audience or a casual, conversational style for a younger demographic. Specify your preferences in your prompt, and ChatGPT will adapt accordingly.

3. Provide examples or references:

   One effective way to guide ChatGPT towards the desired output is by providing examples or references. These can be in the form of similar articles, websites, or even specific phrases you want to include in your content. By offering concrete examples, you can help ChatGPT understand the direction you want the generated content to take.

4. Use the "instruct" function:

   The "instruct" function can be a powerful tool for providing context and detail to ChatGPT. By using phrases like "Imagine you are an expert in X" or "Write as if you were a professional Y," you can set the stage for the AI to generate content from a particular perspective. This approach can be especially useful when you need content that demonstrates a deep understanding of a specific topic or industry.

5. Break down complex tasks:

   When dealing with more complex tasks or multi-part prompts, it's helpful to break them down into smaller, more manageable steps. This approach not only makes it easier for ChatGPT to understand your requirements but also allows you to review and refine the generated content at each stage. For instance, if you need an in-depth article on a specific topic, you could first ask ChatGPT to generate an outline, then request content for each section individually.

6. Experiment with different prompt structures:

   There is no one-size-fits-all solution when it comes to crafting the perfect prompt. Different prompt structures may yield varying results, so it's essential to experiment and find what works best for your needs. For instance, you might find that asking a question produces more engaging content than providing a statement. Don't be afraid to try various approaches and iterate on your prompts until you achieve the desired results.

7. Use prompt limitations to your advantage:

While ChatGPT has a maximum token limit, this constraint can be used to your advantage. By limiting your prompt's length, you can force the AI to generate more concise and focused content. This technique can be especially useful for generating social media posts, ad copy, or other short-form content where brevity is key.

8. Monitor and adjust:
   As you work with ChatGPT, it's essential to monitor the generated outputs and adjust your prompts accordingly. If the content isn't meeting your expectations, consider refining the context or adding more details to your prompt. It's also worth noting that ChatGPT may require a few iterations to produce the desired results, so be patient and persistent in your efforts.

9. Learn from successes and failures:
   As with any tool, mastering ChatGPT requires practice and experimentation. By learning from both successful and unsuccessful attempts, you can refine your approach and develop a deeper understanding of how to provide context and detail effectively. Don't be discouraged by initial setbacks; instead, view them as opportunities to improve your skills and generate better outputs moving forward.

10. Leverage the power of collaboration:
    Lastly, remember that ChatGPT is a powerful collaborative tool. By combining your expertise and knowledge with the AI's vast language model, you can produce content that is both high-quality and uniquely tailored to your needs. Embrace the partnership and use ChatGPT's capabilities to enhance your own creativity and productivity.

In conclusion, providing context and detail is an art that can significantly enhance the quality and relevance of the content generated by ChatGPT. By employing the techniques outlined above, you can ensure that your prompts are clear, specific, and well-structured, allowing the AI to generate content that meets your expectations and aligns with your goals. As you continue to work with ChatGPT, remember to learn from your experiences, iterate on your prompts, and embrace the power of collaboration to make the most of this remarkable tool.

Using the "act like" function and other advanced techniques

As you continue to explore the potential of ChatGPT, you may discover that there are several advanced techniques and functions that can help you generate even more compelling and tailored content. One such feature is the "act like" function, which allows you to instruct ChatGPT to emulate a specific persona or style. In this section, we'll dive into the "act like" function, along with other advanced techniques, to help you unlock the full potential of ChatGPT.

1. The "act like" function:

    The "act like" function is an incredibly powerful tool that allows you to instruct ChatGPT to adopt a specific persona or style. This can be particularly useful when generating content that needs to be aligned with a certain brand voice, target audience, or creative vision. To use the "act like" function, simply include instructions in your prompt, such as "Act like a motivational speaker," or "Act like a scientist explaining a complex concept."

    By providing clear and specific instructions, ChatGPT can generate content that closely aligns with the desired persona or style. For instance, if you're writing a blog post targeting a younger audience, you might instruct ChatGPT to "Act like a popular YouTuber giving advice on personal finance." This will guide the AI to adopt a more casual, engaging tone that resonates with your target demographic.

2. The power of rephrasing:

    Another advanced technique to improve the quality of ChatGPT-generated content is rephrasing your prompts. If the initial output isn't quite what you were looking for, consider rephrasing the prompt to provide a different perspective or angle. For example, if you initially asked ChatGPT to "Explain the benefits of exercise," and the response wasn't satisfactory, you might rephrase the prompt to "Describe the positive effects of regular physical activity on mental and physical health." By doing so, you give ChatGPT another chance to generate content that meets your expectations.

3. Iterative content generation:
   To achieve the best results with ChatGPT, it's often helpful to approach content generation as an iterative process. This involves generating multiple outputs, refining your prompts, and combining the best elements from each iteration to create a final product. For example, you could ask ChatGPT to generate three different opening paragraphs for an article, then choose the one that best aligns with your vision, or even merge elements from all three to create the perfect opening.

4. Prompt chaining:
   Prompt chaining is a technique that involves using the output of one prompt as the input for the next. This can be especially useful when generating long-form content or developing a series of related ideas. By using the output of one prompt as the basis for the next, you can maintain consistency and cohesiveness in your content while still leveraging the power of ChatGPT's language model.

5. Conditional statements:
   When crafting your prompts, consider using conditional statements to guide ChatGPT's responses more effectively. For example, you might say, "If you believe that X is true, explain why. If you believe that X is false, explain why not." By providing conditional instructions, you can generate content that explores multiple perspectives or possibilities, leading to richer, more nuanced outputs.

6. The power of open-ended questions:
   One way to stimulate more creative and engaging content from ChatGPT is to ask open-ended questions. Instead of providing a specific instruction or statement, consider posing a question that encourages the AI to explore various ideas and possibilities. For example, you might ask,

"What are some innovative ways to promote a new product online?" By doing so, you invite ChatGPT to generate a range of creative suggestions and solutions.

7. Experiment with different styles and tones:
   As you work with ChatGPT, don't be afraid to experiment with different styles and tones to discover what resonates best with your audience or aligns with your brand. For instance, you might instruct ChatGPT to generate content in a humorous, informative, or persuasive style. By exploring a variety of approaches, you can hone in on the most effective way to communicate your message and engage your readers.

8. Guiding ChatGPT's focus:
   To ensure that ChatGPT-generated content remains focused on your desired topic, consider providing clear instructions about the scope and focus of your prompt. For example, if you're writing about the benefits of a specific product, you might say, "Discuss the top three benefits of Product X, without mentioning any competitors or unrelated features." This helps to keep the AI's output focused and relevant to your needs.

9. Utilize lists and bullet points:
   When generating content with ChatGPT, consider using lists or bullet points to break down complex ideas or concepts into more digestible and organized formats. By doing so, you can create content that is both easy to read and visually appealing. For example, instead of asking ChatGPT to "Describe the process of creating a marketing plan," you might say, "List the main steps involved in developing a successful marketing strategy."

10. Embrace the power of storytelling:
    One of the most effective ways to engage and connect with your audience is through storytelling. ChatGPT's language model is well-equipped to generate narratives and stories that captivate readers. To leverage this capability, consider providing prompts that encourage

ChatGPT to create compelling stories or anecdotes related to your topic. For example, you might say, "Tell a short story about a small business owner who used social media marketing to transform their business."

In conclusion, the "act like" function and other advanced techniques can significantly enhance the quality, creativity, and effectiveness of the content generated by ChatGPT. By experimenting with different personas, styles, and approaches, you can unlock the full potential of this powerful AI language model and create content that truly stands out. Remember to be patient, persistent, and open-minded as you explore the various techniques and strategies discussed in this section. With practice and persistence, you'll be well on your way to mastering the art of content generation with ChatGPT.

Examples and guidelines for efficient and effective ChatGPT usage

As an AI language model, ChatGPT offers immense potential for generating innovative and engaging content across various platforms. In this section, we will provide examples and guidelines to help you use ChatGPT efficiently and effectively. By following these tips, you'll be able to harness the full power of ChatGPT to create content that is both valuable and captivating.

1. Start with a clear and concise prompt:
   To get the most out of ChatGPT, begin with a clear and concise prompt that outlines your expectations and requirements. This will help the AI understand your needs and generate content that aligns with your goals. For example, instead of saying, "Write about marketing," you might say, "Write a 500-word article about the benefits of content marketing for small businesses."

2. Use open-ended questions:
   When generating content with ChatGPT, consider using open-ended questions to encourage the AI to explore a topic more deeply or creatively. For example, instead of asking, "What is email marketing?" you might ask, "How can businesses benefit from email marketing?" This

will prompt ChatGPT to generate a more in-depth and insightful response.

3. Limit the scope of your prompt:

   While ChatGPT is capable of generating content on a wide range of topics, it's essential to limit the scope of your prompt to ensure that the output remains focused and relevant. For instance, instead of asking, "Write about digital marketing," you might say, "Write a 1000-word article about the importance of SEO in digital marketing."

4. Experiment with different prompt structures:

   To maximize the effectiveness of ChatGPT-generated content, consider experimenting with various prompt structures, such as using lists, bullet points, or subheadings. This will not only help to break up the content into more digestible pieces but also make it more visually appealing. For example, instead of saying, "Write about the benefits of a healthy diet," you might say, "List the top 10 benefits of a plant-based diet."

5. Iterate and refine your prompt:

   If the initial output from ChatGPT doesn't meet your expectations, don't hesitate to iterate and refine your prompt. This could involve rephrasing the question, providing more context, or specifying the desired format or tone. Remember that ChatGPT is a tool, and refining your prompt can help the AI generate content that better meets your needs.

6. Provide examples:

   To help ChatGPT understand the type of content you're looking for, consider providing examples within your prompt. This can be especially useful when requesting specific writing styles or formats. For instance, if you want ChatGPT to generate a persuasive sales pitch, you might include an example of a successful sales pitch within your prompt.

7. Utilize the "act like" function:

When generating content with ChatGPT, consider using the "act like" function to instruct the AI to generate content in the style of a particular person, character, or profession. For example, you might say, "Act like an expert in social media marketing and write a blog post about the latest trends in the industry." This can help to give your content a unique voice and tone.

8. Experiment with temperature and max tokens:
   When using ChatGPT, you can adjust the "temperature" and "max tokens" settings to influence the output. A higher temperature will result in more creative and diverse content, while a lower temperature will produce more focused and conservative responses. Similarly, adjusting the "max tokens" setting can help you control the length of the generated content. Experimenting with these settings can help you fine-tune the AI's output to suit your specific needs.

9. Don't be afraid to edit and revise:
   While ChatGPT is a powerful tool for generating content, it's essential to remember that the AI-generated content might still require editing and revision to meet your standards. Don't be afraid to modify and polish the output as needed to ensure that it is engaging, accurate, and relevant to your audience.

10. Combine AI-generated content with your expertise:
    One of the most effective ways to use ChatGPT is to combine its output with your own knowledge and expertise. For example, you might use ChatGPT to generate a rough draft of an article and then refine it with your own insights and experiences. This approach allows you to harness the AI's speed and efficiency while still maintaining the human touch that makes your content unique and valuable.

11. Use ChatGPT as a brainstorming tool:
    When you're faced with writer's block or need fresh ideas, ChatGPT can be a valuable brainstorming tool. By providing a prompt that encourages

the AI to generate multiple ideas, you can quickly gather a list of potential topics, headlines, or talking points. This can serve as a starting point for your own creative process and help you overcome any barriers to generating new content.

12. Test different outputs:

As you experiment with ChatGPT, don't hesitate to generate multiple outputs for the same prompt. By comparing the results, you can identify the most engaging, relevant, and high-quality content to use for your project. This iterative approach can also help you refine your prompt-writing skills and better understand how to communicate your needs to the AI.

In conclusion, using ChatGPT efficiently and effectively requires a combination of clear communication, experimentation, and iteration. By following these guidelines and examples, you can harness the full potential of ChatGPT to create captivating and valuable content for your audience. Remember that AI-generated content is a tool, and combining it with your own expertise and creativity will lead to the best results.

Chapter 5. Online Course Creation and ChatGPT

Developing course outlines and content with ChatGPT's help

In today's rapidly changing world, education and skill development are paramount. Online courses have become a popular way for people to learn new skills and enhance their knowledge. Developing course outlines and content can be a time-consuming task, but with the help of ChatGPT, you can streamline the process and generate high-quality course materials. In this section, we will discuss various strategies for leveraging ChatGPT to create course outlines and content that are engaging, effective, and tailored to your target audience.

1. Defining your course objectives:

   Before diving into the content creation process, it's essential to clearly define your course objectives. Determine the knowledge or skills you want your learners to acquire and specify the learning outcomes you aim to achieve. Having clear objectives will guide your content development and provide a solid foundation for generating relevant and focused material with ChatGPT.

2. Generating a course outline:

   Once you've established your course objectives, the next step is to create an outline that organizes the course material logically and coherently. To generate a course outline using ChatGPT, provide a prompt that includes the course title, objectives, and desired structure. For example, you might use a prompt like, "Create a course outline for a beginner's guide to digital marketing, including modules on SEO, social media marketing, and email marketing."

3. Building module topics and subtopics:

   After obtaining a high-level outline from ChatGPT, you can further refine the course structure by breaking down each module into specific topics and subtopics. Provide prompts that request the AI to suggest detailed topics and subtopics for each module, ensuring that the content aligns with your course objectives. Remember to iterate and experiment with different prompts to obtain the most relevant and comprehensive results.

4. Generating lesson content and activities:
   With a detailed course structure in place, you can now use ChatGPT to generate content for individual lessons within each module. Craft prompts that ask the AI to provide explanations, examples, and exercises for specific topics. To ensure the content is engaging and interactive, you might also request the inclusion of quizzes, case studies, or practical assignments.

5. Ensuring content accuracy and relevance:
   While ChatGPT is an incredibly powerful tool, it's important to remember that it's not infallible. As a content creator, you must review the AI-generated material for accuracy and relevance. Make any necessary adjustments to ensure that the content aligns with your course objectives and provides the most value to your learners.

6. Incorporating storytelling and real-world examples:
   To make your course content more engaging and relatable, consider incorporating storytelling and real-world examples. Provide prompts that request ChatGPT to generate stories or anecdotes that illustrate key concepts and principles. By connecting abstract ideas to real-life scenarios, you can make the learning experience more enjoyable and memorable for your students.

7. Creating supplementary materials:
   In addition to core course content, supplementary materials such as slide decks, infographics, and worksheets can enhance the learning experience. Use ChatGPT to generate ideas or even draft content for these resources. For instance, you might ask the AI to "Create a summary of the key SEO concepts for a slide presentation" or "Generate a list of practical email marketing tips for an infographic."

8. Adapting content for different learning styles:

   It's important to recognize that learners have diverse learning styles and preferences. To accommodate this, you can use ChatGPT to generate content that caters to different learning modalities, such as visual, auditory, and kinesthetic. Provide prompts that request the AI to create content in various formats, such as videos, podcasts, or interactive exercises.

9. Iterating and refining:

   As with any content creation process, iteration and refinement are essential to producing high-quality course materials. Use feedback from your learners, as well as your own expertise, to identify areas for improvement and make necessary adjustments. Don't hesitate to revisit ChatGPT for additional ideas or content revisions. The more you refine and iterate, the better your course will become.

10. Evaluating course effectiveness:

    To ensure that your course meets its objectives and provides value to learners, it's crucial to assess its effectiveness. Gather feedback from students, track their progress, and analyze the results to determine the impact of your course. This data will inform future revisions and help you optimize your content for maximum efficacy.

In conclusion, ChatGPT is a powerful ally in the process of developing course outlines and content. By providing clear objectives, creating engaging content, and iterating based on feedback, you can produce high-quality educational materials that cater to the needs and preferences of your target audience. Remember to experiment with different prompts and approaches to fully harness the potential of ChatGPT and create a course that truly makes a difference in the lives of your learners.

Strategies for organizing and structuring online courses

Designing and organizing an online course can be a challenging endeavor, particularly for those new to the world of digital education. However, by employing the right strategies and leveraging the power of ChatGPT, you can create a well-structured and engaging learning experience for your students. In this section, we will explore various approaches to organizing and structuring online courses, ensuring that your educational materials are both effective and accessible.

1. Define your course objectives and learning outcomes:
   Before diving into the content creation process, it's essential to establish clear objectives and learning outcomes for your course. This will not only help you maintain focus throughout the development process but also ensure that your students have a clear understanding of what they can expect to gain from the course.

2. Determine the course format:
   Online courses can be delivered in various formats, such as self-paced, instructor-led, or a hybrid of both. Determine the best format for your target audience and the subject matter, taking into consideration factors like learner preferences, engagement levels, and your own availability as an instructor.

3. Break down content into manageable modules:
   Organize your course content into smaller, digestible modules or units. This will make it easier for students to follow along and absorb the material. Consider using a combination of text, video, audio, and interactive elements to cater to different learning styles and keep the content engaging.

4. Develop a logical sequence for content delivery:
   Arrange your course modules in a logical sequence that facilitates knowledge acquisition and skill development. Build on foundational concepts and gradually progress towards more advanced topics, ensuring that students have the necessary background knowledge to fully grasp each new concept.

5. Create engaging and interactive learning activities:
    Incorporate a variety of learning activities throughout your course to promote active engagement and knowledge retention. These may include quizzes, discussion forums, group projects, case studies, or simulations. By providing opportunities for learners to apply their newfound knowledge and skills, you can enhance their overall learning experience.

6. Utilize multimedia elements to enhance content delivery:
    To cater to diverse learning preferences and maintain student engagement, use multimedia elements such as videos, images, and audio recordings to complement your textual content. This will help break up the monotony of long passages of text and make the learning experience more enjoyable.

7. Design clear and concise assessments:
    Assessments play a vital role in evaluating student progress and ensuring that learning objectives have been met. Design assessments that are aligned with your course objectives and learning outcomes, and make sure they accurately measure the knowledge and skills your students have acquired.

8. Establish a system for communication and support:
    To create a sense of community and foster a supportive learning environment, establish clear channels for communication and support. This may involve setting up discussion forums, hosting live Q&A sessions, or providing personalized feedback on assignments. Providing timely and constructive feedback will not only help students feel more connected to the course but also enable them to learn from their mistakes and grow in their understanding.

9. Continuously evaluate and refine your course content:
    Periodically review your course content and make adjustments based on student feedback, learning analytics, and your own observations. By

staying attuned to the needs and preferences of your learners, you can optimize your course for maximum effectiveness and relevance.

10. Provide clear instructions and guidelines:

    To ensure that students can navigate the course effectively and efficiently, provide clear instructions and guidelines throughout the course. This includes outlining expectations for participation, providing guidance on how to access and use course materials, and explaining how assignments should be submitted and graded.

11. Foster a sense of community and collaboration:

    An essential aspect of a successful online course is the sense of community and collaboration among learners. Encourage peer-to-peer interactions through discussion forums, group projects, and other collaborative activities. This not only enhances the learning experience but also helps students build valuable networks and connections.

12. Utilize ChatGPT for content generation and refinement:

    Leverage ChatGPT's capabilities to generate and refine your course content. Whether you need assistance in drafting an engaging course introduction or help in creating quiz questions, ChatGPT can be an invaluable resource. By providing detailed context and specific instructions, you can ensure that the AI-generated content aligns with your course objectives and learning outcomes.

13. Offer supplementary resources and materials:

    To cater to diverse learning needs and preferences, consider providing supplementary resources and materials alongside your primary course content. These might include external articles, videos, podcasts, or other resources relevant to the subject matter. Offering additional materials not only enriches the learning experience but also allows students to explore topics in greater depth and at their own pace.

14. Set clear milestones and deadlines:

    Establishing milestones and deadlines can help students stay on track and manage their time effectively. Make sure to clearly communicate these expectations and provide reminders as needed. Offering flexibility with deadlines can also be beneficial for some learners, as it allows them to work at a pace that suits their individual circumstances.

15. Encourage self-reflection and goal-setting:

    To promote deeper learning and personal growth, encourage students to engage in self-reflection and goal-setting throughout the course. This can be facilitated through activities such as journaling, reflective discussions, or personal development plans. By fostering self-awareness and encouraging students to take ownership of their learning, you can help them achieve their full potential.

In summary, designing a well-structured online course requires careful planning, organization, and execution. By incorporating the strategies discussed in this section and leveraging ChatGPT's capabilities, you can create an engaging and impactful learning experience for your students. Remember, the key to a successful online course lies in being responsive to the needs of your learners and continuously refining your content and delivery methods to provide the most effective and engaging learning experience possible.

Sample prompts for course content generation

To generate course content using ChatGPT effectively, it's essential to provide specific and detailed prompts that align with your course objectives and learning outcomes. Here are some sample prompts (categorized by various content types) that can be used as a starting point for course content generation. Feel free to modify and adapt these prompts to fit your specific course requirements.

1. Course Introduction:

    "Create an engaging course introduction for a beginner's course on digital marketing, highlighting its key topics, learning objectives, and benefits for the learners."

2. Learning Outcomes:

"List and explain five learning outcomes for a course on 'Introduction to Python Programming' targeting beginners with no prior coding experience."

3. Lecture Summaries:

"Write a concise summary for a lecture on 'Search Engine Optimization (SEO)' as part of an online digital marketing course. Include key takeaways and practical tips for learners."

4. Quiz Questions:

"Generate 10 multiple-choice quiz questions for a course module on 'Financial Statement Analysis' in an intermediate-level finance course."

5. Discussion Questions:

"Provide five thought-provoking discussion questions for a course module on 'Ethical Considerations in Artificial Intelligence,' encouraging critical thinking and debate among learners."

6. Assignments:

"Design a group assignment for a course module on 'Brand Strategy' in a marketing course, which requires learners to develop a comprehensive brand strategy for a hypothetical company."

7. Case Studies:

"Write a brief case study on the successful implementation of Agile project management techniques in a software development company, including the challenges faced and lessons learned."

8. Video Script:

"Create a script for a 10-minute explainer video on the topic of 'The Importance of Emotional Intelligence in the Workplace,' targeting professionals looking to improve their interpersonal skills."

9. Reading List:

"Curate a list of five recommended readings (books, articles, or research papers) for a course module on 'Sustainable Business Practices,' including a brief description of each resource and its relevance to the module."

10. Course Wrap-Up:

"Write a course conclusion summarizing the key learnings and encouraging students to apply the knowledge and skills acquired in a course on 'Entrepreneurship and Business Planning.'"

11. Bonus Content:

    "Generate a list of five bonus resources (e.g., articles, videos, podcasts) related to the topic of 'User Experience (UX) Design' that learners can explore for further learning."

12. Infographics:

    "Create an outline for an infographic on 'Top 10 Social Media Marketing Tips for Small Businesses,' including headings and key points for each tip."

13. Webinar Topics:

    "Propose three engaging webinar topics related to 'Leadership and Management' that would be suitable for an online course aimed at new and aspiring managers."

14. Expert Interviews:

    "Write a list of 10 questions for an interview with a renowned expert in the field of 'Data Science and Machine Learning,' focusing on practical advice and insights for learners."

15. Course Assessments:

    "Design a final assessment for a course on 'Public Speaking and Presentation Skills,' which tests learners' abilities to effectively plan, structure, and deliver a persuasive presentation."

16. Course Feedback and Evaluation:

    "Create a feedback form to assess the effectiveness and overall satisfaction of participants who completed a 'Social Media Marketing' course, including questions about the course content, instructor's teaching style, and practical application of learned skills."

17. Content Creation Techniques:

    "Write a step-by-step guide on creating engaging and informative video content for a course on 'Graphic Design Fundamentals,' including tips on selecting appropriate visuals, narrating effectively, and maintaining viewer interest."

18. Time Management Skills:

"Develop a lesson plan for a course module on 'Time Management Strategies for Entrepreneurs' that covers essential techniques such as prioritization, goal setting, and effective use of technology to boost productivity."

19. Negotiation Skills:

"Outline a role-playing exercise for a course on 'Advanced Negotiation Techniques' that simulates a high-stakes business negotiation, requiring learners to utilize persuasive communication, active listening, and creative problem-solving skills."

20. E-commerce Fundamentals:

"Design a series of practical assignments for a course on 'Starting an E-commerce Business' that guide students through the process of choosing a niche, creating a business plan, setting up an online store, and marketing their products."

21. Personal Branding:

"Craft a series of exercises for a course on 'Building a Powerful Personal Brand' that help learners identify their unique strengths, develop a compelling story, and create a consistent online presence across various platforms."

22. Networking Strategies:

"Develop a hands-on activity for a course on 'Effective Networking for Professionals' that encourages participants to practice their elevator pitch, engage in meaningful conversations, and cultivate long-term relationships."

23. Conflict Resolution:

"Outline a case study for a course on 'Workplace Conflict Resolution' that presents a challenging interpersonal conflict scenario, prompting learners to analyze the situation, identify underlying issues, and propose a constructive resolution."

24. Search Engine Optimization (SEO):

"Create a practical exercise for a course on 'SEO for Small Businesses' that guides students through the process of optimizing their website's content and structure to improve search engine rankings and drive organic traffic."

25. Public Relations Strategies:

"Design a group project for a course on 'Public Relations for Startups' that tasks learners with developing a PR strategy for a fictional company, including crafting a press release, identifying target media outlets, and pitching their story."

26. Data Analysis and Visualization:

"Develop a series of interactive assignments for a course on 'Data Analysis and Visualization with Python' that cover essential skills such as data cleaning, statistical analysis, and creating visually appealing charts and graphs."

27. Freelancing and Remote Work:

"Write a comprehensive guide for a course on 'Thriving as a Freelancer' that includes tips on finding clients, setting rates, managing time and resources, and maintaining a healthy work-life balance."

28. Leadership and Team Building:

"Outline a series of group activities for a course on 'Leadership and Team Building' that help learners practice effective communication, collaboration, and decision-making skills in a dynamic team environment."

29. Customer Service Excellence:

"Design a role-playing exercise for a course on 'Delivering Exceptional Customer Service' that simulates a challenging customer interaction, requiring learners to demonstrate empathy, active listening, and effective problem-solving."

30. Digital Marketing Strategies:

"Create a comprehensive project for a course on 'Digital Marketing for Beginners' that requires learners to develop an integrated marketing plan, including SEO, content marketing, social media, and email marketing strategies."

These sample prompts can serve as a foundation for generating various types of course content using ChatGPT. Remember to provide sufficient context and be as specific as possible to guide the AI in generating content that aligns with your course objectives and learning outcomes. Experiment with different prompt structures and techniques to find what works best for your unique requirements. By harnessing the power of ChatGPT, you can create engaging and impactful course content, enhancing the overall learning experience for your students.

Chapter 6. Ebooks, Guides, and Reports

Leveraging ChatGPT to create comprehensive and informative documents

As the digital age continues to advance at a rapid pace, the need for creating comprehensive and informative documents has become more crucial than ever. ChatGPT, a state-of-the-art language model, is an incredibly valuable resource for authors and content creators looking to produce high-quality ebooks, guides, and reports. By utilizing ChatGPT's powerful features and capabilities, one can create engaging, well-structured documents that effectively convey their intended message and appeal to their target audience.

One essential aspect of leveraging ChatGPT for document creation is understanding the model's ability to grasp context and generate content based on the given prompts. By providing detailed and specific instructions, users can access ChatGPT's vast knowledge base to gather relevant information, generate concise summaries, and even brainstorm potential topics for their document. This not only saves time but also ensures comprehensive coverage of the subject matter, resulting in a more informative and well-rounded document.

Additionally, ChatGPT can be utilized to create a detailed outline or structure for the document, making it easier for authors to organize their thoughts and maintain a logical flow. By providing a preliminary outline or a list of headings, users can prompt ChatGPT to expand on each section, generating content that aligns with the desired structure. This step-by-step process allows authors to refine their document's organization, ensuring a coherent narrative that effectively communicates the intended message.

Apart from providing valuable information, ChatGPT can also help authors develop a unique and engaging writing style tailored to their specific audience. By experimenting with various tones, sentence structures, and vocabulary choices, users can customize their document's language to align with their target demographic. This ensures that the content resonates with readers, holds their attention, and encourages them to continue reading.

Another critical aspect of creating comprehensive and informative documents is the integration of data, statistics, and research findings to support arguments and assertions. ChatGPT's extensive knowledge base allows it to provide relevant data points, research results, and statistics that pertain to the subject matter. This feature not only enhances the credibility of the document but also lends authority to the author's voice, making it more persuasive and compelling.

When it comes to crafting informative documents, maintaining consistency in terminology and formatting throughout the text can be challenging. ChatGPT can help achieve consistency by generating content that adheres to user-defined guidelines. For instance, if a specific abbreviation or technical term is preferred, users can specify this preference in their prompt, ensuring that the AI-generated content maintains a uniform style.

Furthermore, ChatGPT's ability to generate content in multiple languages can be invaluable for businesses and individuals looking to reach a global audience. By providing prompts in the desired language, users can access a wealth of information and generate content that is both accurate and culturally sensitive. This enables them to create localized versions of their ebooks, guides, and reports that cater to diverse readerships around the world.

Another advantage of using ChatGPT for document creation is its capacity for iterative improvement. Users can leverage the AI's capabilities to proofread their content, correct grammatical errors, and enhance readability. This iterative process ensures that the document is not only comprehensive and informative but also professionally presented and free of errors.

In addition to proofreading and polishing the final document, ChatGPT can be employed to generate various types of content, such as case studies, white papers, and industry-specific reports. By providing targeted prompts, users can access ChatGPT's domain-specific knowledge, resulting in content that is both insightful and relevant to the target audience.

Lastly, one of the most significant benefits of using ChatGPT for creating ebooks, guides, and reports is the time and effort saved by authors and content creators. The AI's ability to generate content quickly and efficiently allows them to focus on refining their ideas, researching additional information, and polishing their final product. This increased efficiency enables authors to produce high-quality documents in a fraction of the time it would take using traditional methods, allowing them to stay ahead of the curve and meet tight deadlines with ease.

In conclusion, leveraging ChatGPT to create comprehensive and informative documents offers numerous advantages for authors and content creators. From generating well-structured outlines and engaging content to providing relevant data points and maintaining consistency, ChatGPT is an invaluable tool for producing ebooks, guides, and reports. Its ability to adapt to different writing styles, languages, and subject matter ensures that users can create content tailored to their specific audience, resulting in a more impactful and persuasive document.

By harnessing the power of ChatGPT, authors can streamline their content creation process, ensuring that their final product is not only informative but also engaging and professionally presented. With the AI's assistance, authors can overcome common challenges associated with document creation, such as writer's block, maintaining a consistent tone, and organizing complex information.

As technology continues to evolve, the possibilities for AI-assisted content creation are virtually limitless. By staying informed about the latest advancements in AI technology and learning how to use tools like ChatGPT effectively, authors and content creators can remain competitive in an increasingly digital landscape. By embracing the power of ChatGPT, they can produce comprehensive and informative documents that resonate with their target audience, ensuring their message is heard loud and clear.

Ebooks, Guides, and Reports

Writing and editing ebooks and reports can be a daunting task, especially for those new to the process or dealing with complex subject matter. However, with the help of advanced AI tools like ChatGPT, authors can streamline their workflow and produce high-quality documents that captivate their target audience. This paragraph will delve into various techniques for writing and editing ebooks and reports, offering valuable insights for authors looking to create comprehensive, informative, and engaging content.

One of the most critical aspects of writing an ebook or report is proper planning and organization. Begin by outlining the content, creating a structure that will guide the reader through the material in a logical and coherent manner. ChatGPT can assist authors in generating a well-structured outline, providing a solid foundation for the document. Additionally, by breaking the content down into smaller sections or chapters, the author can more easily manage the writing process, tackling one section at a time.

Research is another essential component of creating an informative and accurate document. ChatGPT can be utilized to gather relevant data and information on a specific topic, helping authors to bolster their content with facts and statistics that support their arguments. However, it's crucial to verify the information provided by the AI, cross-referencing with reliable sources to ensure accuracy.

When writing the content, authors should focus on maintaining a consistent style and tone throughout the document. This consistency is vital for fostering reader engagement and ensuring that the material is easily digestible. ChatGPT can be tailored to match the desired writing style and tone, allowing authors to create content that resonates with their target audience. However, it's important to remember that the AI-generated content should be thoroughly reviewed and revised as needed to ensure it aligns with the author's voice and message.

Another technique to consider is the use of storytelling and real-life examples to illustrate key points and concepts. By incorporating relatable anecdotes and case studies, authors can create a more engaging and persuasive narrative, helping readers to better understand and retain the information presented. ChatGPT can be an invaluable resource for generating compelling examples and stories, but it's important to ensure that these elements are relevant and accurate, enhancing the overall quality of the document.

When it comes to editing the ebook or report, it's crucial to approach the task with a critical eye, meticulously reviewing the content for clarity, coherence, and consistency. Authors should carefully examine the document's structure, ensuring that it flows smoothly and logically from one section to the next. Additionally, they should assess the relevance and accuracy of the information provided, making necessary revisions to enhance the overall credibility and persuasiveness of the content.

ChatGPT can be a helpful tool during the editing process, providing suggestions for revisions and improvements. However, it's essential for authors to maintain a discerning perspective, carefully considering the AI's recommendations and making adjustments based on their judgment and expertise. This collaborative approach can lead to a more polished and impactful final product, ensuring that the document meets the highest standards of quality and professionalism.

In addition to using ChatGPT for editing assistance, authors may also consider collaborating with professional editors or proofreaders to further refine their work. These experts can provide valuable insights and recommendations, helping authors to fine-tune their content and eliminate errors in grammar, punctuation, and syntax. By enlisting the help of professionals, authors can ensure that their document is not only informative but also well-written and engaging.

In conclusion, the process of writing and editing ebooks and reports can be significantly enhanced with the help of AI tools like ChatGPT. By harnessing the power of this technology, authors can more efficiently plan, research, and write their content, creating documents that are both informative and engaging. Furthermore, with the AI's assistance during the editing process, authors can refine their work to achieve a higher level of quality and professionalism, ultimately resulting in a more impactful and valuable final product.

One aspect of creating successful ebooks and reports is incorporating visually appealing elements, such as images, graphs, and charts, to supplement the text. These visual aids can help to break up large blocks of text, making the content more accessible and engaging for readers. ChatGPT can assist in generating ideas for visual aids, but it's essential to source high-quality images and create accurate and visually appealing graphs or charts to maintain a professional appearance.

Additionally, formatting plays a crucial role in the overall presentation and readability of an ebook or report. Authors should pay close attention to typography, spacing, and layout, ensuring that the content is easy to read and navigate. ChatGPT can provide guidance on formatting best practices, but it's vital for authors to review the final document on various devices and platforms to ensure a consistent and user-friendly experience for all readers.

When finalizing an ebook or report, authors should also consider the importance of an eye-catching cover design and a compelling title. These elements play a significant role in attracting potential readers and setting the tone for the content within. ChatGPT can be used to generate ideas for titles and cover designs, but authors may also wish to consult with professional designers or conduct market research to ensure their choices resonate with their target audience.

Lastly, it's essential for authors to develop a comprehensive marketing and distribution strategy for their ebooks and reports. This may involve leveraging social media platforms, creating engaging promotional content, and identifying appropriate distribution channels. ChatGPT can assist in generating marketing ideas and content, but authors should also consider their unique audience and goals when developing a tailored strategy for promoting their work.

In summary, the process of writing, editing, and publishing ebooks and reports can be greatly enhanced with the support of AI tools like ChatGPT. By leveraging this advanced technology, authors can create well-structured, informative, and engaging content that resonates with their target audience. Furthermore, with careful attention to detail in editing, formatting, and design, authors can ensure their work meets the highest standards of quality and professionalism, ultimately resulting in a more successful and impactful final product.

Sample prompts for generating ebooks, guides, and reports in the "make money" niche

In the ever-evolving world of making money online, generating ebooks, guides, and reports can provide valuable insights and strategies for those looking to diversify their income streams. By using ChatGPT, authors can create compelling and informative content that addresses various aspects of this lucrative niche. The following sample prompts can be used as a starting point for generating ebooks, guides, and reports tailored to the "make money" niche:

1. Passive Income Strategies:
    "Outline a comprehensive guide that explores various passive income strategies, including affiliate marketing, dividend investing, and real estate crowdfunding, explaining the benefits and drawbacks of each approach."
2. Building a Profitable Blog:
    "Develop a detailed ebook that walks readers through the process of starting, growing, and monetizing a blog, covering topics such as niche selection, content creation, search engine optimization, and affiliate partnerships."
3. E-commerce Success:
    "Write a step-by-step guide that explains how to launch a successful e-commerce business, from product selection and sourcing to marketing, customer service, and fulfillment."
4. Freelancing for Beginners:
    "Create a comprehensive report that delves into the world of freelancing, covering essential topics such as setting rates, finding clients, marketing services, and managing projects effectively."
5. Cryptocurrency Investment:

"Craft an informative ebook that demystifies cryptocurrency investment for beginners, explaining the basics of blockchain technology, popular cryptocurrencies, and strategies for building a diversified portfolio."

6. Online Course Creation:

"Develop a guide that outlines the process of creating and selling online courses, touching on topics such as course planning, content creation, pricing, and marketing."

7. Social Media Monetization:

"Write a report that explores the various ways individuals can monetize their social media presence, including sponsored posts, affiliate marketing, and selling digital products."

8. Stock Market Investing:

"Create a comprehensive ebook that introduces readers to the world of stock market investing, covering key concepts such as fundamental analysis, technical analysis, and portfolio diversification."

9. Dropshipping Business:

"Outline a step-by-step guide that teaches aspiring entrepreneurs how to launch and operate a successful dropshipping business, covering aspects such as niche selection, supplier partnerships, and marketing strategies."

10. Self-publishing for Profit:

"Develop a detailed report that delves into the world of self-publishing, offering practical advice on writing, editing, formatting, and marketing a self-published book for maximum profit."

11. Amazon FBA Business:

"Craft a comprehensive guide that provides a detailed overview of building a successful Amazon FBA business, discussing essential aspects such as product research, sourcing, listing optimization, and advertising strategies."

12. YouTube Monetization:

"Develop an informative ebook that explores the various ways to monetize a YouTube channel, including ad revenue, sponsored content, and digital product sales, while sharing tips on video creation, audience engagement, and channel growth."

13. Affiliate Marketing Mastery:

"Write a step-by-step guide that delves into the world of affiliate marketing, covering topics such as choosing a niche, selecting affiliate programs, creating engaging content, and driving targeted traffic to maximize conversions."

14. Trading Forex for Profit:

"Create a comprehensive report that introduces readers to the world of forex trading, discussing key concepts such as currency pairs, leverage, technical analysis, and risk management, along with proven strategies for long-term success."

15. Email Marketing for Beginners:

"Outline a detailed ebook that teaches aspiring digital marketers how to build and grow a profitable email list, covering topics such as lead generation, email copywriting, and automation tools for effective campaign management."

16. Podcasting for Profit:

"Develop a guide that explores the various ways to monetize a podcast, including sponsorships, donations, and digital product sales, while sharing insights on recording, editing, and promoting podcast episodes for maximum reach."

17. Mastering Membership Sites:

"Write an informative report that delves into the world of membership sites, providing practical advice on selecting a profitable niche, creating valuable content, and engaging members for long-term success and recurring revenue."

18. NFT Investing and Trading:

"Create a comprehensive ebook that introduces readers to the exciting world of NFT investing and trading, covering key concepts such as blockchain technology, popular NFT marketplaces, and strategies for identifying and acquiring valuable digital assets."

19. Mobile App Monetization:

"Outline a step-by-step guide that teaches aspiring app developers how to monetize their mobile apps, discussing essential aspects such as app store optimization, in-app advertising, and in-app purchases for maximizing revenue."

20. Mastering Etsy Selling:

"Develop a detailed report that explores the world of Etsy selling, offering practical advice on product selection, pricing, listing optimization, and marketing strategies for both physical and digital products."

By leveraging these sample prompts, authors can create comprehensive and engaging content that caters to the needs and interests of readers within the "make money" niche. It's essential to tailor the content to the target audience, providing actionable advice, real-life examples, and case studies that inspire and educate. Furthermore, using ChatGPT's advanced language capabilities, authors can generate content that is both informative and enjoyable to read, ensuring that their ebooks, guides, and reports stand out in a competitive marketplace.

Chapter 7. Email Marketing and ChatGPT

Utilizing ChatGPT for crafting engaging email sequences

In today's competitive digital landscape, creating engaging email sequences that capture your audience's attention and prompt them to take action is a critical aspect of successful email marketing. ChatGPT can be an invaluable tool in crafting compelling email sequences that resonate with your subscribers, keep them engaged, and ultimately drive results for your business.

To leverage ChatGPT effectively in your email marketing strategy, it is essential to understand its capabilities and limitations. ChatGPT can generate creative and persuasive content based on the prompts you provide, making it a powerful ally in your email marketing efforts. However, it is also essential to fine-tune and tailor the generated content to your specific audience and goals.

To begin, let's explore the different stages of crafting an engaging email sequence using ChatGPT.

1. Research and planning: To create an email sequence that resonates with your target audience, you must first understand their needs, preferences, and pain points. Utilize ChatGPT to conduct market research by generating interview questions, survey prompts, and other types of content that can help you gather valuable insights about your target audience. These insights will serve as the foundation for your email sequence.

2. Setting objectives: With a clear understanding of your audience, define the objectives of your email sequence. These objectives should align with your overall marketing goals and guide the content of your emails. Examples of objectives include nurturing leads, promoting a product or service, or driving engagement with your brand. Use ChatGPT to generate content ideas that align with your objectives and resonate with your audience.

3. Crafting compelling subject lines: The subject line is the first thing your subscribers see when they receive your email, and it plays a crucial role in determining whether they open it. Use ChatGPT to generate multiple subject line options for each email in your sequence. Experiment with different styles, such as using questions, personalization, or urgency, to capture your audience's attention. Remember to A/B test your subject lines to determine which ones perform best.

4. Creating engaging email content: Once you have your subject lines in place, it's time to craft the body of your emails. Use ChatGPT to generate content ideas, and structure your emails in a way that guides your subscribers through the sequence. Keep your audience's preferences and pain points in mind while writing, and make sure your content aligns with your email sequence's objectives. Utilize storytelling, personalization, and persuasive writing techniques to keep your subscribers engaged and encourage them to take action.

5. Call-to-action (CTA): Every email in your sequence should include a clear and compelling call-to-action that directs your subscribers to take a specific action, such as clicking a link, making a purchase, or signing up for a webinar. Use ChatGPT to generate persuasive CTA copy that aligns with your email's objectives and your audience's needs.

6. Reviewing and editing: Before sending your emails, it's crucial to review and edit the content generated by ChatGPT. While the AI can produce high-quality content, it is still essential to ensure the content is free from errors, aligns with your brand voice, and effectively communicates your message. Review the content for grammar, syntax, and overall coherence, and make any necessary revisions to ensure it meets your standards.

7. Testing and optimization: After you've crafted your email sequence, it's essential to test and optimize it to maximize its effectiveness. Monitor the performance of your emails, including open rates, click-through rates, and conversions, and use this data to identify areas for improvement.

Experiment with different subject lines, content styles, and CTAs to determine what resonates best with your audience, and make data-driven decisions to optimize your email sequence further.

In conclusion, ChatGPT can be a powerful tool in crafting engaging email sequences that drive results for your business. By leveraging the AI's capabilities in generating creative and persuasive content, you can develop email campaigns that resonate with your audience and prompt them to take action. However, it's crucial to remember that the AI-generated content should be fine-tuned and tailored to your specific audience and goals.

Utilize ChatGPT effectively by conducting research and planning, setting clear objectives, crafting compelling subject lines and email content, incorporating persuasive calls-to-action, and reviewing and editing the content before sending it out. Continuously test and optimize your email sequences based on performance data, making data-driven decisions to improve the effectiveness of your campaigns.

By combining the power of ChatGPT with a strategic approach to email marketing, you can create captivating email sequences that keep your subscribers engaged, build lasting relationships, and ultimately drive success for your business. So, harness the potential of ChatGPT and elevate your email marketing game to new heights.

Strategies for maximizing open rates and click-through rates

In the world of email marketing, maximizing open rates and click-through rates (CTRs) is a top priority for marketers, as it can significantly impact the success of campaigns. To make the most out of your email marketing efforts, it's essential to implement effective strategies that boost these critical metrics. In this section, we will delve into various tactics that can help you achieve higher open rates and CTRs.

1. Personalization and segmentation: One of the most effective ways to increase open rates and CTRs is by personalizing and segmenting your email campaigns. By tailoring your messages to individual subscribers,

you can create a more meaningful connection with your audience. Segment your email list based on factors like demographics, location, interests, and behavior to deliver more relevant content. For example, you can address recipients by their first name or create content based on their browsing history, which will make them feel valued and increase the chances of engagement.

2. Compelling subject lines: A well-crafted subject line can make or break your email's success. It's the first thing recipients see and often determines whether they will open the email or not. To maximize open rates, create enticing subject lines that pique curiosity and create a sense of urgency. Experiment with different styles like asking a question, using numbers, or incorporating power words to see what works best for your audience. Keep in mind that brevity is key - aim for 50 characters or less to ensure your subject lines are fully visible on mobile devices.

3. Preheader text optimization: Preheader text, also known as the email preview, appears next to or below the subject line in most email clients. By optimizing this text, you can provide additional context and encourage recipients to open your email. Make sure to use the preheader text to complement the subject line and provide a brief summary of the email's content. Avoid using generic phrases or repeating the subject line, as it can make your email seem less appealing.

4. Mobile-friendly design: With a significant portion of email opens happening on mobile devices, it's crucial to ensure your emails are mobile-friendly. Optimize your email design for smaller screens by using responsive templates, clear and concise copy, and large, easily clickable buttons. Test your emails on various devices and email clients to ensure they render correctly and provide a seamless experience for all users.

5. Consistent and valuable content: To maintain high open rates and CTRs, consistently deliver valuable content that resonates with your audience. Focus on providing relevant information, tips, or resources that address

their needs or interests. By offering value, you'll build trust and credibility, which will encourage subscribers to engage with your emails and look forward to receiving them.

6. Optimal send times: Timing can play a significant role in the success of your email campaigns. To increase open rates, experiment with different send times and days of the week to determine when your audience is most likely to engage with your content. Monitor your email analytics and look for patterns in engagement to fine-tune your send schedule. Keep in mind that optimal send times may vary depending on factors like your industry, target audience, and the type of content you're sending.

7. Clear and concise calls-to-action (CTAs): To maximize CTRs, use clear and concise CTAs that prompt subscribers to take a specific action. Ensure your CTA buttons are visually distinct and placed prominently within the email. Limit the number of CTAs in each email to avoid overwhelming your audience and focus on one primary action you want them to take.

8. A/B testing: Continuously test various elements of your email campaigns to identify what resonates best with your audience and drives higher engagement. Some aspects you can test include subject lines, preheader text, send times, content layout, and CTA formatting, and CTA placement. By regularly conducting A/B tests, you can gather valuable insights that will help you optimize your email strategy and achieve better results.

9. Regular list hygiene: Maintaining a clean email list is essential for maximizing open rates and CTRs. Regularly remove inactive subscribers, invalid email addresses, and hard bounces to ensure your list remains up-to-date and engaged. Doing so will also help you avoid potential deliverability issues and maintain a strong sender reputation.

10. Establishing trust and credibility: Building a strong relationship with your subscribers is crucial for maintaining high open rates and CTRs. Be transparent about who you are and why you're emailing them. Use a recognizable sender name and consistently deliver high-quality content that aligns with your brand's identity. By establishing trust and credibility, you'll increase the likelihood of subscribers opening and engaging with your emails.

11. Monitor and analyze performance: Keep a close eye on your email marketing metrics to identify trends, areas for improvement, and successes. Regularly analyze open rates, CTRs, bounce rates, and unsubscribe rates to gain insights into your audience's preferences and behavior. Use this data to make informed decisions about your email marketing strategy and adapt your approach as needed.

12. Encourage social sharing: Including social sharing buttons in your emails can help increase engagement and visibility. Encourage subscribers to share your content with their networks by making it easy for them to do so. This not only increases the reach of your content but also has the potential to attract new subscribers who may be interested in what you have to offer.

In conclusion, maximizing open rates and click-through rates is essential for the success of your email marketing campaigns. By implementing these strategies, such as personalization, segmentation, crafting compelling subject lines, and consistently delivering valuable content, you can boost engagement and drive better results for your business. Remember, email marketing is a continuous process of learning and adapting, so make sure to monitor your performance and make adjustments as needed to ensure you're consistently meeting your audience's needs and preferences.

Sample prompts for various types of email campaigns

In the realm of email marketing, there are various types of email campaigns that cater to different objectives and target different segments of your audience.

Crafting a compelling message for each campaign type is crucial for achieving your marketing goals. To assist you in this endeavor, here are some sample prompts for various types of email campaigns. These prompts can serve as a starting point, helping you to create tailored content that resonates with your subscribers and drives the desired results:

1. Welcome email series: Crafting an engaging welcome email series is essential for building a strong relationship with new subscribers from the very beginning. Here are some sample prompts to help you create an effective welcome email sequence:
   - "Introduce your brand's mission, values, and unique selling points in a warm and engaging manner."
   - "Provide subscribers with an overview of the types of content they can expect to receive from your newsletter and the frequency of your emails."
   - "Offer a special discount, exclusive content, or free resource as a thank you for joining your list."

2. Abandoned cart recovery emails: These emails aim to re-engage customers who have left items in their online shopping cart without completing their purchase. Sample prompts for abandoned cart emails include:
   - "Remind the customer of the items they left in their cart and offer a time-sensitive discount to encourage them to complete their purchase."
   - "Highlight the unique features or benefits of the products in the cart, emphasizing why they are worth purchasing."
   - "Address potential objections or concerns that may have prevented the customer from completing their purchase, such as shipping costs, payment options, or return policies."

3. Product launch emails: When introducing a new product or service, your email campaign should generate excitement and anticipation among your subscribers. Here are some sample prompts for product launch emails:

- "Describe the main features and benefits of the new product or service, emphasizing how it solves a specific problem or meets a particular need."
- "Share customer testimonials or case studies that demonstrate the effectiveness and value of the new product or service."
- "Offer a limited-time promotion or exclusive bonus for early adopters to encourage immediate action."

4. Re-engagement emails: Reconnecting with inactive subscribers requires a different approach than engaging with active subscribers. Sample prompts for re-engagement emails include:

   - "Acknowledge the subscriber's inactivity and express your desire to rekindle the relationship, inviting them to share their preferences or reasons for disengagement."
   - "Curate a selection of your most popular or valuable content since their last interaction, demonstrating what they may have missed out on."
   - "Offer a special incentive or exclusive content as a way to encourage them to re-engage with your brand."

5. Upsell and cross-sell emails: Encouraging existing customers to purchase additional products or services can be an effective strategy for increasing revenue. Sample prompts for upsell and cross-sell emails include:

   - "Recommend complementary products or services that enhance or complement the customer's previous purchase."
   - "Share the benefits of upgrading to a higher-tier plan or package, highlighting the additional features or perks they would receive."
   - "Provide a limited-time offer or promotion to incentivize the customer to make an additional purchase."

6. Educational content emails: Providing valuable information and resources to your subscribers can help build trust and loyalty. Sample prompts for educational content emails include:

   - "Share actionable tips, tricks, or best practices related to your industry or niche."

- "Offer in-depth guides, case studies, or research findings that can help subscribers better understand a specific topic or issue."
- "Invite subscribers to attend webinars, workshops, or other educational events hosted by your brand."

These are just a few examples of the types of email campaigns you might create as part of your overall email marketing strategy. By using these sample prompts as a starting point, you can develop compelling email content that resonates with your subscribers and drives your desired results. Remember to always consider the unique needs and preferences of your target audience, and continually test and refine your messaging to optimize your email campaigns for maximum impact.

Chapter 8. ChatGPT and Affiliate Marketing

How ChatGPT can support affiliate marketing efforts

In the competitive world of affiliate marketing, leveraging advanced tools and technologies such as ChatGPT can provide a significant edge. ChatGPT, with its powerful language understanding and generation capabilities, can support various aspects of an affiliate marketer's efforts, from content creation to audience engagement and conversion optimization. In this comprehensive guide, we will delve into the numerous ways ChatGPT can bolster affiliate marketing strategies, ensuring that marketers are equipped with the necessary tools and insights to achieve success.

First and foremost, content creation is a critical component of any affiliate marketing strategy. High-quality, engaging, and informative content is essential to attract and retain potential customers. ChatGPT can assist in generating blog posts, product reviews, comparison articles, and other types of content that can seamlessly incorporate affiliate links. By providing ChatGPT with specific prompts, marketers can obtain unique and relevant content tailored to their target audience, saving time and effort while still delivering value to readers.

Moreover, ChatGPT can be used to craft compelling headlines and meta descriptions that can drive organic traffic to the affiliate marketer's website. With the right balance of creativity and keyword optimization, these elements can improve search engine rankings and increase the visibility of the marketer's content, resulting in higher click-through rates and potential conversions.

Another area where ChatGPT can be immensely valuable is in creating engaging social media content. Affiliate marketers can use the AI to generate captivating social media posts, captions, and even responses to comments and messages, allowing them to maintain a consistent and active presence across various platforms. By crafting personalized and engaging content that resonates with the target audience, marketers can foster a sense of community and brand loyalty, increasing the likelihood of conversions and repeat customers.

Email marketing, as we discussed in the previous chapter, is also a crucial aspect of many affiliate marketing campaigns. ChatGPT can aid in crafting persuasive and engaging email sequences, from welcome emails to promotional campaigns and follow-up messages. By utilizing the AI's language generation capabilities, marketers can optimize open rates, click-through rates, and conversions, ensuring a higher return on investment for their email marketing efforts.

Furthermore, ChatGPT can support the creation of advertising copy for various platforms, such as Google Ads, Facebook Ads, or native advertising networks. Crafting compelling ad copy that captures the attention of potential customers while adhering to platform-specific guidelines can be challenging. ChatGPT can simplify this process by generating creative, persuasive, and compliant ad copy that encourages users to click through and explore the marketer's content.

In addition to content creation, ChatGPT can also provide valuable insights and suggestions for optimizing affiliate marketing campaigns. By analyzing existing content and offering recommendations for improvement, the AI can help marketers fine-tune their strategies and achieve better results. For example, ChatGPT can suggest ways to optimize content structure, incorporate relevant keywords, or even address potential customer objections and concerns, ensuring that the marketer's content is as persuasive and effective as possible.

Finally, ChatGPT can be a useful tool for conducting research and staying informed about the latest trends and developments in the affiliate marketing industry. By providing the AI with relevant prompts, marketers can obtain curated summaries, reports, and analyses of industry news, competitors' strategies, and emerging opportunities. This valuable information can enable affiliate marketers to make informed decisions and stay ahead of the curve in an ever-evolving landscape.

In conclusion, ChatGPT's language understanding and generation capabilities offer a powerful resource for affiliate marketers looking to streamline their content creation efforts, engage their audience effectively, and optimize their campaigns for maximum conversions. By leveraging this advanced tool, affiliate marketers can save time, effort, and resources while still delivering high-quality, targeted content that drives results. With the ongoing advancements in AI technology, ChatGPT's role in affiliate marketing is poised to grow, providing even greater benefits to marketers seeking to stay competitive and achieve success in their niche.

Additionally, ChatGPT can be an invaluable asset in the process of selecting and promoting the most suitable affiliate products or services for a specific target audience. By analyzing the audience's preferences, needs, and pain points, the AI can provide tailored recommendations on which products or services to promote, ensuring that the marketer's content remains relevant and valuable to readers.

Moreover, ChatGPT can assist affiliate marketers in creating high-converting landing pages and sales funnels. By generating persuasive copy, engaging visuals, and optimized calls-to-action, the AI can help ensure that potential customers who click on affiliate links are directed to well-designed, compelling pages that encourage conversions.

Beyond content and promotion, ChatGPT can also be utilized for monitoring and analyzing the performance of affiliate marketing campaigns. By providing insights into key performance indicators (KPIs) such as traffic, engagement, click-through rates, and conversions, the AI can help marketers identify areas of improvement and make data-driven decisions to optimize their strategies.

Furthermore, ChatGPT can be a useful resource for networking and relationship-building within the affiliate marketing industry. By generating personalized outreach messages and follow-up communications, the AI can assist marketers in forging valuable connections with other industry professionals, influencers, and potential partners. These relationships can lead to mutually beneficial collaborations, increased exposure, and new opportunities for growth.

Affiliate marketers can also benefit from ChatGPT's capabilities in creating educational and training resources, such as ebooks, guides, and online courses, to help them stay up-to-date with the latest industry best practices and strategies. These resources can not only serve as valuable learning tools for the marketers themselves but can also be used as lead magnets or bonuses to attract new subscribers and customers.

In summary, ChatGPT's wide-ranging capabilities make it an indispensable tool for affiliate marketers looking to improve their content creation, audience engagement, campaign optimization, and overall marketing strategy. By leveraging the power of AI, affiliate marketers can stay ahead of the competition, maximize their ROI, and achieve greater success in an increasingly competitive landscape. As AI technology continues to advance and evolve, we can expect even more innovative applications and opportunities for ChatGPT in the realm of affiliate marketing, empowering marketers to reach new heights of success.

Techniques for creating content that promotes affiliate products effectively

Creating content that effectively promotes affiliate products is an essential skill for affiliate marketers who want to maximize their revenue and build lasting relationships with their audience. By employing a mix of proven techniques and innovative strategies, marketers can generate persuasive, engaging, and informative content that drives conversions and boosts their bottom line. In this section, we will discuss several key techniques for creating compelling content that effectively promotes affiliate products, ensuring that your marketing efforts yield optimal results.

1. Understanding your audience: The foundation of any successful affiliate marketing campaign is a deep understanding of your target audience. Research their demographics, preferences, pain points, and motivations to ensure that your content resonates with them on a personal level. Tailor your messaging, tone, and style to suit their preferences and create a sense of trust and rapport that encourages them to take action.

2. Providing value: To effectively promote affiliate products, your content should focus on providing value to your audience. This can be achieved by offering insightful information, practical advice, or actionable solutions to their problems. By positioning yourself as an expert in your niche and demonstrating the benefits of the product or service you are promoting, you can build credibility and persuade your audience to click on your affiliate links.

3. Storytelling: Harness the power of storytelling to create content that engages your audience on an emotional level. Share personal anecdotes, case studies, or success stories that demonstrate the effectiveness of the affiliate product in solving a particular problem or improving a specific aspect of life. By connecting with your audience through relatable stories, you can create a compelling narrative that drives conversions.

4. Transparency and authenticity: Be transparent about your relationship with the affiliate product or service you are promoting. Clearly disclose your affiliate partnership and maintain an authentic, unbiased tone in your content. This builds trust with your audience and ensures that they view your recommendations as genuine and credible.

5. Balance promotion with education: While your primary goal may be to generate conversions, it's crucial to strike a balance between promotional content and educational material. Offer a mix of product-focused content, such as reviews and comparisons, alongside more general, informative pieces that address broader topics within your niche. This approach helps maintain audience engagement and positions you as a knowledgeable resource in your industry.

6. Utilizing multiple content formats: To maximize the reach and effectiveness of your affiliate marketing efforts, experiment with a variety of content formats, such as blog posts, videos, podcasts, and social media updates. This allows you to cater to diverse audience preferences and increase the likelihood of your content being discovered and shared.

7. Strong calls-to-action (CTAs): Guide your audience towards conversion with clear, compelling calls-to-action. Make your CTAs highly visible, using contrasting colors, bold text, or eye-catching graphics, and ensure that your messaging is persuasive and action-oriented. This helps to create a sense of urgency and encourages your audience to click through to the affiliate product or service.

8. SEO optimization: Optimize your content for search engines by conducting keyword research and incorporating relevant keywords and phrases throughout your text, headings, and metadata. This increases the visibility of your content in search engine results and helps to drive targeted, organic traffic to your affiliate links.

9. Testing and analytics: Regularly track and analyze the performance of your content using tools such as Google Analytics or dedicated affiliate marketing software. Identify which content formats, topics, and promotional strategies generate the highest engagement and conversion rates, and use this data to inform your future content creation efforts.

10. Continuous improvement: Stay up-to-date with industry trends, best practices, and emerging technologies to ensure that your content remains fresh, relevant, and effective. Regularly update and improve your existing content to maintain its value and appeal to both your audience and search engines.

By employing these techniques and maintaining a consistent, audience-focused approach, affiliate marketers can create content that effectively promotes their chosen products and generates significant revenue. Keep in mind that successful affiliate marketing requires patience, persistence, and ongoing experimentation, so be prepared to adjust your strategies as needed and learn from your successes and failures.

11. Engaging visuals: Enhance your content by incorporating engaging visuals, such as images, infographics, or videos. This not only helps to break up large blocks of text, making your content more digestible, but also provides additional value and context for your audience. High-quality visuals can help illustrate key concepts, showcase the features and benefits of the product, and make your content more shareable on social media platforms.

12. Collaborate with influencers: Partner with influencers in your niche to broaden the reach of your content and tap into new audiences. Influencers can help promote your content and affiliate products through guest posts, social media shoutouts, or product reviews, leveraging their established credibility and following to drive traffic and conversions.

13. Leverage user-generated content: Encourage your audience to share their experiences with the affiliate products by creating user-generated content (UGC), such as testimonials, case studies, or social media posts. This not only fosters a sense of community and engagement among your audience but also provides valuable social proof that can influence purchasing decisions.

14. Consistency and scheduling: Maintain a consistent posting schedule to keep your audience engaged and build anticipation for your content. Develop a content calendar that outlines your planned content topics, formats, and publishing dates, and stick to this schedule as closely as possible. Consistency helps establish your authority within your niche and keeps your audience coming back for more.

15. Cross-promotion and repurposing: Maximize the reach and impact of your content by cross-promoting it across multiple platforms and channels. Share your blog posts on social media, turn articles into video scripts, or transform a series of related posts into a comprehensive ebook

or guide. Repurposing your content allows you to cater to diverse audience preferences and extend the shelf life of your content.

In conclusion, crafting engaging content that effectively promotes affiliate products requires a strategic, audience-focused approach that combines valuable information, authentic storytelling, and persuasive calls-to-action. By employing the techniques outlined in this article, affiliate marketers can develop a loyal and engaged audience, drive conversions, and ultimately achieve their revenue goals. Remember, success in affiliate marketing requires ongoing learning and adaptation, so stay committed to refining your strategies and exploring new opportunities to grow your business.

Sample prompts to generate affiliate marketing content

Affiliate marketing is an ever-evolving industry that demands creativity and innovation to generate compelling content that effectively promotes products and services. As a ChatGPT-4 expert and writer, I am pleased to provide you with sample prompts that can help you generate a wide range of affiliate marketing content. These prompts will not only spark ideas for informative and engaging content but also demonstrate how to utilize ChatGPT effectively to streamline your content creation process. So, let's dive into the world of affiliate marketing with these carefully curated sample prompts, and remember to experiment with different content formats to cater to your audience's diverse preferences.

1. "Write a comprehensive review of [Product Name], highlighting its features, benefits, and potential drawbacks, as well as comparing it to similar products in the market."
   This prompt encourages a detailed analysis of a specific product, providing valuable information for potential buyers and establishing your authority in the niche.

2. "Create a step-by-step tutorial on how to use [Product Name] to solve a common problem or achieve a specific goal."

This type of content showcases the practical applications of a product and demonstrates its value to potential customers.

3. "Compile a list of the top 10 [Product Category] products for [Target Audience], including a brief description and unique selling points for each item."
   Listicles are highly popular among online audiences, and this format allows you to promote multiple affiliate products in a single piece of content.

4. "Share a personal success story of how [Product Name] helped you overcome a challenge or achieve a significant milestone."
   Authentic, relatable stories can resonate with your audience and build trust in your recommendations.

5. "Interview an expert in the [Niche] field, discussing the benefits of [Product Name] and its relevance in the industry."
   Expert opinions can lend credibility to your content and provide additional insights into the product's value proposition.

6. "Write a case study that highlights how [Product Name] has helped a customer achieve their goals or overcome a specific obstacle."
   Case studies provide concrete examples of a product's effectiveness, offering valuable social proof to potential buyers.

7. "Craft an email newsletter that shares valuable tips and insights related to [Niche], with strategic mentions of [Product Name] and its benefits."
   Email newsletters are an excellent way to nurture your audience and promote affiliate products in a non-intrusive manner.

8. "Develop a series of social media posts that showcase the various features of [Product Name] through eye-catching images, informative captions, and persuasive calls-to-action."

Leveraging social media can help you reach a broader audience and generate interest in your affiliate products.

9. "Create an infographic that visually explains the key features and benefits of [Product Name], and how it compares to other products in the market."
Infographics are an engaging way to convey complex information in a visually appealing and easily digestible format.

10. "Write a script for a video review of [Product Name], discussing its pros and cons, demonstrating its use, and sharing personal experiences or testimonials."
Video content is highly popular and can be a powerful tool for promoting affiliate products.

11. "Design a quiz or interactive tool that helps users determine the best [Product Category] product for their specific needs, leading them to your recommended affiliate product."
Interactive content can engage your audience and help them make informed decisions about the products they're considering.

12. "Craft a series of blog posts that explore various aspects of [Product Name] in depth, providing valuable insights and practical advice for users."
Creating a series of related blog posts can help establish your authority in the niche and provide ample opportunities to promote your affiliate products.

13. "Write an ultimate guide to [Niche Topic], incorporating expert advice, helpful tips, and strategic mentions of relevant affiliate products."
Ultimate guides can position you as a go-to resource in your niche and offer numerous opportunities to promote affiliate products within valuable, in-depth content.

14. "Curate a collection of user-generated content, such as testimonials, reviews, and success stories, highlighting the real-life impact of [Product Name]."

    User-generated content can serve as powerful social proof and show potential customers how the product has positively affected others in similar situations.

15. "Develop a comprehensive resource hub that covers various topics related to [Niche], with a dedicated section for recommended affiliate products."

    A resource hub can provide valuable information to your audience while seamlessly integrating your affiliate product recommendations.

16. "Craft a series of guest posts for industry-leading blogs, discussing trending topics in your niche and subtly mentioning relevant affiliate products."

    Guest posting on authoritative websites can help you reach new audiences and promote your affiliate products in a natural, non-promotional manner.

17. "Design an engaging webinar or online workshop that teaches a specific skill or shares valuable insights related to [Niche], while strategically promoting relevant affiliate products."

    Webinars and workshops are effective ways to engage with your audience and showcase your expertise, while also promoting your affiliate products.

18. "Create a podcast series that covers various topics within your niche, inviting industry experts to discuss their experiences and insights, and promoting relevant affiliate products."

    Podcasts are a popular content format that can help you connect with your audience on a deeper level and promote your affiliate products through engaging conversations.

19. "Develop a free e-book or lead magnet that provides valuable information related to [Niche], with strategic mentions of your recommended affiliate products."

Free resources like e-books or lead magnets can help you grow your email list and introduce your audience to your affiliate product recommendations.

20. "Write a press release announcing the launch of [Product Name], highlighting its innovative features and benefits, and sharing quotes from industry experts who endorse the product."

Press releases can generate media coverage and buzz around a new product, which can translate into increased interest and potential sales through your affiliate links.

These 20 sample prompts offer a wide range of possibilities for generating engaging and persuasive affiliate marketing content that effectively promotes your chosen products. By leveraging the power of ChatGPT and incorporating these prompts into your content creation process, you can streamline your efforts and consistently produce high-quality content that resonates with your audience and drives results for your affiliate marketing campaigns.

Conclusion

Throughout this comprehensive guide, we've explored the incredible potential of ChatGPT and how it can revolutionize your business, streamline your content creation process, and enhance your marketing efforts. From social media content, blog posts, and email campaigns to affiliate marketing, course creation, and ebooks, ChatGPT's versatility knows no bounds, offering you a powerful tool to supercharge your content production.

In Chapter 1, we introduced you to the basics of ChatGPT, discussing its origins, functionality, and how it operates. You learned how this AI-driven language model generates human-like text and the importance of using effective prompts to guide its output, providing you with the desired results.

In Chapter 2, we delved into the world of social media and ChatGPT, covering strategies to generate engaging social media content that resonates with your audience. We provided valuable tips and sample prompts to guide your social media content creation and demonstrated how ChatGPT can be a game-changer in managing your online presence.

Chapter 3 took us on a journey into the realm of blogging and website content. You discovered techniques for crafting compelling blog posts, creating outlines, and producing high-quality content with the assistance of ChatGPT. We also shared sample prompts to help you create captivating content for your website that keeps your readers hooked and coming back for more.

Chapter 4 focused on the power of ChatGPT in the online course creation process, showcasing how it can assist you in developing course outlines, content, and assessments. You learned strategies for organizing and structuring online courses, as well as numerous sample prompts to help you generate course content tailored to your needs.

In Chapter 5, we turned our attention to ebooks, guides, and reports, demonstrating how ChatGPT can aid you in creating comprehensive, informative documents. We discussed techniques for writing and editing these long-form materials, and provided a wealth of sample prompts for generating content in various niches, including the lucrative "make money" niche.

Chapter 6 tackled the world of email marketing and how ChatGPT can be harnessed to craft engaging email sequences that resonate with your subscribers. We discussed strategies for maximizing open rates and click-through rates, and provided an array of sample prompts for different types of email campaigns.

In the penultimate chapter, Chapter 7, we explored the synergy between ChatGPT and affiliate marketing. We unveiled how ChatGPT can support your affiliate marketing efforts, and shared techniques for creating content that effectively promotes affiliate products. The chapter also included sample prompts designed to help you generate a wide range of affiliate marketing content.

As we conclude this guide, it's essential to remember that the true power of ChatGPT lies in its ability to learn and adapt. By taking the time to understand the nuances of this AI-driven language model and tailoring your prompts to your specific needs, you can unlock a world of possibilities for your business.

Now, it's your turn to harness the power of ChatGPT and elevate your content creation process to new heights. The future of content marketing is here, and it's time for you to embrace it. By leveraging the tips, strategies, and sample prompts provided in this guide, you can streamline your content production, engage your audience, and drive tangible results for your business.

Don't wait another moment to start using ChatGPT in your content creation workflow. The sooner you begin, the sooner you'll reap the benefits of this innovative, powerful tool. With ChatGPT by your side, you'll be well on your way to achieving your content marketing goals and taking your business to the next level. So go ahead, dive into the world of ChatGPT, and watch your business soar!

Appendix A – Bonus 1000 Impressive ChatGPT Prompts

We're happy to give you access to 1000 exclusive ChatGPT prompts as a special thank you for buying this book. These prompts can help you utilize ChatGPT to its greatest potential for your company. Simply scan the QR-code provided in this book to get your bonus. With these well created prompts at your disposal, you'll have a priceless toolkit that can help you come up with original ideas, improve marketing tactics, produce top-notch content, and grow your company to new heights. Don't pass up this fantastic chance to accelerate your path to success in the "make money" sector!

Also 2 more bonuses for you, so that you can apply ChatGPT to financial freedom and e-commerce.

Printed in Great Britain
by Amazon